King Lear

WILLIAM SHAKESPEARE

Guide written by

Stewart Martin

A *Lett* Guide

First published 1995
Reprinted 1998
This edition revised by Ron Simpson

Letts Educational
Aldine House
Aldine Place
London W12 8AW
0181 740 2266

Text © Stewart Martin 1995

Typeset by Jordan Publishing Design

Text design Jonathan Barnard

Cover and text illustrations Hugh Marshall

Design © BPP (Letts Educational) Ltd

Acknowledgements

Outline answers are solely the responsibility of the author, and are not supplied or approved by the Exam Board.

British Library Cataloguing in Publication Data
A CIP record for this book is available from the British Library

ISBN 1 85758 269 1

Printed and bound in Great Britain
Ashford Colour Press, Gosport, Hampshire

Letts Educational is the trading name of BPP (Letts Educational) Ltd

Contents

Plot synopsis   4

Who's who in *King Lear*   5

Themes in *King Lear*   14

Text commentary Act One   17

Self-test questions Act One   27

Text commentary Act Two   28

Self-test questions Act Two   34

Text commentary Act Three   35

Self-test questions Act Three   43

Text commentary Act Four   44

Self-test questions Act Four   52

Text commentary Act Five   53

Self-test questions Act Five   58

How to write a coursework essay   60

How to write an examination essay   64

Self-test answers   66

◼ Plot synopsis

Lear, King of Britain, decides to give up the royal power in view of his great age, though retaining the name of King. He plans to divide his kingdom between his three daughters: Goneril (married to the Duke of Albany), Regan (married to the Duke of Cornwall) and Cordelia (whose hand is sought in marriage by the Duke of Burgundy and the King of France). He invites each of his daughters to gain a larger share by declaring how much she loves him. Goneril and Regan make extravagant claims; Cordelia refuses and is disinherited. The Earl of Kent is banished for disagreeing with Lear, but soon returns to serve him in disguise. Cordelia leaves England with her new husband, the King of France. Before long Lear has a violent disagreement with Goneril about his knights and goes to stay with Regan.

The Earl of Gloucester's illegitimate son, Edmund, has been plotting to betray his half-brother Edgar and take his inheritance. By means of a forged letter and a fake attack he convinces Gloucester that Edgar intends to murder him. Gloucester makes Edmund his heir; Edgar flees, disguised as a wandering madman.

Regan has moved to Gloucester's castle and there Lear finds that both she and Goneril insist that he dismiss his soldiers. Lear leaves in a fury, encountering the disguised Edgar in a violent storm on the heath. Gloucester has corresponded with Cordelia and learns that a French army has arrived at Dover to rescue Lear from the ingratitude of Goneril and Regan. Gloucester helps Lear to escape, but is betrayed to Regan and her husband, the Duke of Cornwall, by Edmund. Cornwall blinds Gloucester for his treachery, but is then fatally wounded himself by a servant. Gloucester is led by the disguised Edgar to Dover, where Edgar forestalls his attempted suicide.

Cordelia, who has arrived with a French army, is reconciled with Lear, but in the ensuing battle with Edmund's forces they are defeated and both are imprisoned. In a series of dramatic events a succession of deaths follows. Goneril poisons Regan, her rival for Edmund's love, then commits suicide. Edgar challenges Edmund in combat and kills him, revealing that Gloucester has died on discovering Edgar's identity. Cordelia has been hanged on Edmund's orders and Lear's heart breaks in the hope that she still breathes. Albany leaves the kingdom in the hands of Kent and Edgar, although Kent does not expect to live long.

King Lear

As the play begins, Lear is King of Britain. At over eighty years of age, he is a very old man and has decided to give up the cares of being monarch and to divide his kingdom between his three daughters. He rejects his youngest daughter, Cordelia, when she refuses to copy her sisters in their exaggerated declarations of love for him. However, after the kingdom is divided between his other two daughters, Goneril and Regan, he finds that they want nothing further to do with him. Lear goes mad as he considers the damage he has brought upon himself, but in his madness he undergoes a period of examination both of himself and of Mankind in general. He learns the power of love and forgiveness at the same time as he realises what a poor, frail thing Man is. Unfortunately, by the time he recovers into something approaching sanity, he no longer has the physical vitality to sustain life.

At the start of the play, Lear is a proud old man. He expects everyone, even his own grown-up children, to obey him in everything – including a charade of flattery so that he may decide on a whim which of them is to receive the greater part of his kingdom. His judgement at the start of the play is consistently faulty, not only in the division of the kingdom, but in his understanding of other characters' motives, such as Kent who is banished for being too honest. His provocative behaviour towards his daughters and their households is equally foolish and based upon his unawareness of his own weakness. Lear's sufferings reveal to him the truth about himself and other people, as he joins the outcasts of society: Kent, Edgar, Gloucester, the Fool, finally Cordelia.

The storm which marks the height of his rage symbolises the conflict in the play between madness and reason, order and disorder. Lear breaks the natural order by dividing his kingdom, rejecting his responsibilities and his daughter. For this, he is made to suffer until he is partly redeemed at the end of the play, but not before he has paid a terrible price.

Cordelia

Cordelia

The third of Lear's three daughters and the most virtuous, Cordelia is the catalyst both for the action of the tragedy and for its conclusion. We may wonder why, at the start of the action, she does not humour her father more but she shares some of his stubbornness and cannot bear false shows of affection. Her abiding honesty, so lacking in her father's view of himself, is what makes her the symbol of hope in the play. Cordelia leaves Britain with the King of France at the end of the first scene in Act 1 and we do not see her again until she returns with a rescuing army in Act 4. By the end of the play she, like her father, has mellowed and seeks reconciliation; both have put all past resentment behind them. Cordelia and Lear are captured in battle by the wicked Edmund, who plans their murder, and Cordelia is killed before Edgar and his followers can prevent it. Lear has come to realise that Cordelia is the one great jewel left in his life and her death therefore removes his only remaining reason for existence.

Cordelia's central part in the drama is remarkable, considering how infrequently we see her. She appears in only 4 of the play's 26 scenes and has only about 100 lines to say, but Shakespeare skilfully employs other devices to keep her in the audience's mind and she is referred to frequently at key moments. In particular, the disguised Kent is her representative in Britain and constant evidence both of her plans and of her goodness. Shakespeare's presentation of symbolic goodness is all the more effective because of her comparatively few appearances and few words. Cordelia's relative silence contrasts strongly with the rest of the play, with the power of its language and the richness of its imagery. Her silence also reinforces her character's dramatic function as a Christian metaphor for the spiritual silence and calm at the centre of life's storm.

Cordelia has often been seen as a personification of self-sacrifice and the passive acceptance of God's will, which were deemed as great Christian virtues at the time. Another view of the play argues that *King Lear* is exactly what it appears to be, a depressing and soul-destroying view of human existence which sees no hope for forgiveness or happiness. In such a view Cordelia's goodness and her death merely serve to underline the way any hope for the human spirit will always be snuffed out by the essential wickedness and stupidity of humankind.

Goneril and Regan

Lear's other two daughters reflect the more vicious side of his character. They represent the damage done when a kingdom (or a king) is turned against itself. They are also the instruments of their own destruction, for like Lear they lack self-knowledge; but unlike him their destruction is not tragic, for they are no wiser by the end of the action and their wickedness is revealed as a form of ignorance and spitefulness.

Although Goneril and Regan both declare their wholehearted love for their father, they in fact want only his land and power. Goneril is the leading activist in the humiliation of Lear. It is she who begins the argument about how many of Lear's knights he really needs and it is this which precipitates his fleeing in a rage into the gathering storm and into madness. Goneril is also guilty of adultery (with Edmund) and there are hints of a plot between the two of them to murder her husband, the Duke of Albany.

Goneril and Regan each wants the corrupt and scheming Edmund for herself and these three characters emphasise the moral and sexual corruption which runs through the play. Eventually the plot against the Duke of Albany is uncovered and Goneril poisons her sister, then commits suicide. The two sisters are similar in many ways, although Goneril dominates her husband, whilst Regan tends to be led by hers. They are really distinguished by the more extreme evil of the cruel and ambitious Goneril; Regan urges her husband, the evil Cornwall, to hang Gloucester for helping

Lear, but it is Goneril who suggests that instead Cornwall should pluck out his eyes. Goneril and Regan behave in an unnatural way towards their father and each other; often they are described in terms of animal images – such as wolves and tigers – which emphasise their greedy and vicious natures.

Edmund

Edmund

Edmund, the illegitimate son of the Earl of Gloucester, is calculating, cruel and merciless. He betrays the Earl's legitimate son Edgar, having falsely accused him of plotting against his father's life. He also betrays the Earl of Gloucester to Regan and her husband the Duke of Cornwall. Edmund's taste for betrayal even extends to matters of love, where he plots with Goneril to take the life of Albany and inspires her to fatal jealousy by also seeking the love of Regan. These events all contribute to the play's emphasis on moral and political disintegration.

In the last act of the play Edmund leads the army against Cordelia's forces, who have come to rescue Lear. When Edmund is victorious, he imprisons Cordelia and her father and schemes to have them both murdered. When his plot against the Duke of Albany is discovered, Edmund is accused of treason and, in a fight with Edgar, is fatally wounded. He confesses to plotting against Cordelia and Lear but it is too late to save Cordelia, whose murder causes her father to die of a broken heart.

Edmund is a type often to be found in Elizabethan and Jacobean drama: the Machiavellian villain. Machiavelli's book, *The Prince*, laid down rules and gave guidance for ruling effectively, but the Elizabethan playwrights concentrated solely on the elements of scheming and manipulation to create an unprincipled villain. Edmund seems a more modern figure than his brother, whose chivalric virtue seems to him merely foolish. Note that Edmund, while deceiving the other characters, reveals his self-knowledge to the audience in a soliloquy early in the play. Edmund finally attains some element of honour in his actions in the duel with Edgar and his attempt to save Cordelia.

Edgar

Edgar

Edgar is the legitimate son of the Earl of Gloucester, who is betrayed by his illegitimate brother Edmund and then banished by his father. This banishment is a parallel of Cordelia's rejection by Lear and both the king and Gloucester are blind – in several senses – to the real qualities of those around them. In fear of arrest and death, Edgar disguises himself as a wandering madman, Tom O'Bedlam. In this disguise, he later meets up again with Lear after Goneril and Regan have refused to house him. Later still, Edgar meets his now blinded father and becomes his guide, although Gloucester does not recognise him. He accompanies Gloucester to Dover and prevents his attempted suicide. By the end of the play Edgar has exposed Goneril and Edmund's evil plot to murder Albany. Edgar kills Edmund and becomes one of those appointed to rule Britain.

Edgar's love for his father echoes that of Cordelia for Lear in the same way that his pretended madness, when he is Tom O'Bedlam, parallels the real madness of the king. Tom O'Bedlam and Cordelia both exhibit saintly characteristics and are willing to sacrifice themselves for their fathers. In the role of Tom, Edgar acts as a guide and saviour both for Gloucester and Lear. At the end of the play he is cast in the same light in relation to the kingdom as a whole. As Tom O'Bedlam, Edgar also becomes the living example of the play's themes of disease and misery as the results of human foolishness. He says his mad and beggarly state is due to his sexual misbehaviour. This parallels Lear's condemnation of procreation and woman's role in this as contributing factors to his own fate. At the end of the play, Edgar says that Edmund's wickedness is attributable to his bastard origin in lust – completing a reference made at the start of the play, where Gloucester says that Edmund was conceived as a result of sexual gratification and not from a loving marriage.

Edgar acts as a link between the play's main plot and its sub-plot – between the story of Lear and his trouble-filled kingdom and Edmund's plotting for the physical conquest of the kingdom and the moral conquest of the old order of values. Edgar does not subscribe to or exhibit any corrupt values. His main role is to act as a positive force for goodness as a balance to Edmund's motiveless evil. Edgar has many roles to fulfil and is therefore – like many characters in the play – as important for what he represents as for his personal growth or character.

The Earl of Gloucester

The Earl of Gloucester banishes his legitimate and loving son, Edgar, whilst accepting his illegitimate and evil son, Edmund, in a way which mirrors Lear's rejection of Cordelia. As a weak reflection of Lear, Gloucester is the central figure in the sub-plot. He falls prey to Edmund's lies and manipulation and although well-meaning, he is a morally weak man. At the start of the play he brushes off his promiscuous relationship with Edmund's mother, although in the past he has felt guilty about it. Although not a character who takes a great moral lead publicly, Gloucester does stand up for what is right against the forces of evil, as represented by Goneril and Cornwall, and for this he is cruelly blinded. After this Gloucester wishes to end his life, seeing himself as a victim of fate's cruelty, like Lear. He fails to see any connection between his own past behaviour and his own suffering.

Although Edmund is wicked, it is Gloucester's own mistakes which bring disaster upon him. He suffers and partly recovers but, like Lear, dies before the end of the action. Gloucester is physically blinded by the Duke of Cornwall in the same way that Lear is emotionally blinded, but through the suffering caused by this both men achieve a clearer vision of the world around them and those within it, especially their children. Gloucester is blinded to the goodness in Edgar by Edmund's deceits and follows the latter's plans without ever taking the initiative himself – he seems swept along by events, rather than one in control of his own destiny. It is tempting to think of Gloucester's punishment as something which he is destined to suffer because of his lust and the resultant birth of Edmund, but equally we can see that it is a result of his blindness to Edmund's real character. Gloucester has hardened himself to his own feelings so that he can now accept Edmund, but this proves to be his undoing. At the end of the play, Gloucester is a sadder and wiser man who dies because he cannot reconcile his joy at being reunited with Edgar with his feelings of guilt at the wrongs he has done to him.

The Earl of Kent

As Lear's loyal servant, Kent tries to persuade him not to deal harshly with Cordelia when she refuses to swear her love for him. For this Kent suffers the same fate as Cordelia and is banished, but he disguises himself so that he may continue to serve the king. This connects him with the play's themes of reality and self-knowledge, although unlike Edgar, Kent reappears as essentially himself. He protects Lear from rumoured attempts on his life and plays a part in reuniting the king with Cordelia at the end of the play. Kent makes no secret of being a blunt and forthright dealer with others – even with his master Lear – and often his inability to control his temper lands him in trouble. He is a man of unhesitating action. He abuses the servant Oswald and beats him violently for being disrespectful to Lear and it is this which leads to Kent being put in the stocks by Cornwall in Act 2, scene 2. Kent is unchanging; always the steadfastly virtuous and honest servant, whose sufferings and impending death at the end of the play emphasise the play's sense of the nobility of human suffering.

The Fool

Although a traditional figure in contemporary drama, and one used frequently by Shakespeare, the Fool in *King Lear* is special in being almost a shadow of the king himself. He appears after Lear has divided his kingdom and vanishes from the action when Lear travels to Dover. In a play where so many characters are not what they appear, the Fool pretends to be what he is not, in his professional capacity as an entertainer. Through his songs, riddles and jokes he tries to get Lear to see the truth of the world around him. Like many others in the play, the Fool is important not so much as a character, as for the dramatic function which he fulfils. He acts in some ways as a chorus in commenting upon the action of the play, but does so in a pointed and witty way.

The Fool is identified with Cordelia on a number of occasions and pines for her when she is away. He knows that Lear was wrong to reject Cordelia in favour of Goneril and Regan and keeps reminding him of his foolishness. After Lear goes mad, the Fool stays with him and touchingly tries to protect him and guide him to shelter from the storm. Like Kent and Cordelia, the Fool is a voice of common sense and sanity and he is loyal to Lear throughout, although he disappears in Act 3. His fate in uncertain. Lear, near to death, says that his 'poor fool' is hanged, but this is often taken to mean Cordelia, 'fool' meaning 'innocent'. However, hanged or not, it is difficult to imagine the Fool surviving hunger, the storm and Edmund's forces.

The Duke of Albany

The Duke of Albany is Goneril's virtuous but weak and fallible husband. He is at first ruled completely by his wife. When he discovers the extent of Goneril's wickedness, he rounds on her and helps to restore Lear to power. In this way, Albany stands alongside the other characters who affirm the importance of moral growth. At the end of the play he is one of those who will rule the kingdom and bring back justice and order. We might wonder, however, how much Albany has learned from what has happened, for he divides the rule of the kingdom at the end of the play in a way which echoes the foolishness of Lear at the beginning.

The Duke of Cornwall

The Duke of Cornwall is the husband of Regan. He is a violent and cruel man who is completely without any redeeming features. He has violent rages and is often involved in the destructive and evil actions which occur in the play. He puts Kent in the stocks even though he knows he is acting as the King's messenger and that doing so is a huge insult to Lear. He joins forces with Goneril and Regan in their attempt to usurp Lear. He passes a death sentence on the innocent Edgar and, after gouging out Gloucester's eyes with his own hands, installs the wicked and deceitful Edmund as Earl of Gloucester in his father's place. For this

Cornwall pays with his life, killed by one of his own servants who is outraged at the blinding of Gloucester. His conduct during the play is a graphic example of the destruction which is released in the world when reason, order and obedience are overthrown.

The King of France

At the start of the play, France accepts Cordelia as his wife without Lear's blessing of a dowry. He says that she 'is herself a dowry', emphasising one of the play's most important ideas; that the outward appearance of deeds and words should not automatically be taken for truth. By having France take Cordelia back home with him, Shakespeare removes her from most of the play's action and thereby absolves her of any responsibility for the actions of her two sisters. At the end of the play, France's men arrive to rescue Lear but, significantly, France himself is called back home urgently. This device is dramatically useful because it leaves Cordelia's part in the redemption of Lear undiluted by her husband's presence.

Themes and images in King Lear

Love

Love

Edgar's and Cordelia's feelings for their respective fathers are characterised by love, loyalty and affection. The children act as examples of how the great power of love can redeem even these two foolish old men. Through the suffering which their own blindness to real love has brought upon them, both Lear and Gloucester slowly and painfully come to appreciate the true qualities of those around them and learn to change. At the start of the play Gloucester expects, and Lear demands, that their children respect and honour them out of a sense of duty. These two men represent the traditional view which emphasises the individual's acceptance of his/her place in the world. Sadly, however, Lear and Gloucester have forgotten that their expectations of filial obedience and loyalty should be accompanied by accepting and loving others in return.

Gloucester's lustful urges are as misplaced as Lear's tyrannical demands for power without responsibility; both generate offspring who attempt to destroy them. Goneril, Regan and Edmund are the embodiments of the self-destructive elements in Lear and Gloucester. This expresses itself in the play as the conflict between what they expect of others and what those around them – especially their children – expect in return. As the play opens, both Gloucester and Lear are preoccupied with their own selfish feelings and it is not until they begin to learn from their suffering that they can appreciate and find a way to accept the unconditional love of others. This love is expressed through the way Edgar and Cordelia cherish and support their parents, accept them for what they are and their offences. It is equally but differently expressed through the unswerving loyalty of the Fool and Kent, who act as examples of the personal and political loyalty and affection which is offered to Lear but is not always appreciated by him. The way Edgar and Cordelia forgive their fathers marks the climax of the theme of love in the play. The destructive spite which erupts between Goneril and Regan over their feelings for Edmund annihilates them both – it is founded upon a desire for possession, not on love; significantly, Edmund feels nothing for either of them. Whilst Goneril, Regan and Edmund die in hatred and frustration, Lear, Cordelia and Gloucester die surrounded by love, acceptance and reconciliation.

Order and reason

Order and reason

In Shakespeare's time, many people believed that the monarch ruled by divine right and was the voice of God on earth. The monarch represented only one aspect of an ordered universe which encompassed all things both living and inanimate. Everything had its place in a hierarchy of importance which led from stones through the plant and animal world to humankind, then the angels and, at the summit, God. To disturb this ordered structure was to invite chaos into the world. Many of Shakespeare's plays concern themselves with the consequences of the overthrowing of kings; perhaps a reflection of the Elizabethan Age's anxieties over who would succeed to the throne after the death of the virgin Queen Elizabeth I.

Lear's renunciation of the throne and the dividing of his kingdom would, therefore, have seemed incomprehensible to Elizabethan audiences, although some of them would have sympathised with his sense of frustration at having no son to succeed him. But for Shakespeare's contemporaries, Lear had only one option – he should see out his God-given task to the end, not seek to evade his responsibilities because of personal considerations.

The play is full of references to heavenly order and prayers. Several times characters refer to the gods above as watching and judging the actions of humans below. The idea that heavenly justice will descend upon the wrongdoers becomes more noticeable as the play nears its end. But the justice which Edgar sees the gods dispensing is also accompanied by great human suffering. Lear is not the only character to assume (mistakenly) that the gods are on his side, as we see in the scene where he sets up court and tries Goneril and Regan in what is, in several ways, a mockery of justice.

Blindness and sight

Blindness and sight

The way in which seeing clearly is linked to an understanding of what the world is really like is an idea which appears again and again throughout the play. It surfaces in the many references to metaphorical and literal blindness, as well as in references to moral 'blindness' or depravity. Other imagery – notably that about animals – supports this notion by contrasting the behaviour of humankind with that of beasts. Shakespeare continually reworks the imagery so that it both illustrates and becomes the vehicle for expressing the dramatic structure of the play. For example, references to blindness and sight work through images of animals and the natural order of the universe to find an expression in other images about self-knowledge, personal identity and the theme of disguise. The revealing to Lear of who he really is is a painful learning process which requires him to shed those things which on the surface seem often to express the inner self – rich clothing, fine speech, obedient-seeming behaviour of children, the courtly deference of a servant. Lear has to shed his sanity and descend to nakedness in the storm to reach some understanding of the nature of humankind. Gloucester has to be physically blinded before he can see the world more nearly as it is. Lear's madness destroys his ability to make sense of the world but out of his spiritual and moral blindness he emerges as one who has, through his suffering, gained greater insight.

Essays

This icon is used throughout the **Text commentary** to draw attention to material that should be of particular relevance to the section on **How to write a coursework essay**. Each time it is used, it is accompanied by a note that identifies which essay title the material relates to and adds a relevant comment, quotation or piece of advice.

■ Text commentary

Act 1 Scene 1

In King Lear's palace, the Earl of Gloucester, accompanied by his illegitimate son Edmund, discusses with the Earl of Kent Lear's plans to divide his kingdom. King Lear enters with his daughters Goneril, Regan and Cordelia. Goneril is accompanied by her husband the Duke of Albany; Regan by her husband the Duke of Cornwall. Lear announces that Cordelia's hand is being sought by the King of France and the Duke of Burgundy. He asks his daughters to tell him how much they love him, so that he may give the greatest share of his kingdom to the one who loves him most. Goneril and Regan flatter their father with exaggerated speeches of love, but Cordelia says only that she loves her father and will love her husband when she marries. Lear becomes furious, disowns Cordelia and banishes Kent when he intervenes to defend her. Burgundy refuses to accept Cordelia now that she is disinherited, but the King of France says he will marry her and take her back to his own country. Left alone together, Goneril and Regan agree that their father has become infirm and troublesome and that they must act together to deal with him.

'Is not this your son, my Lord?'

Kent's question to Gloucester contains an unconscious irony, one which is all

the more significant for appearing only a few lines into the play. Edmund is indeed not what he seems and so is linked immediately with concepts of appearance and reality, blindness and sight. Edmund is handsome, sexually attractive (especially to Goneril and Regan) and on the surface appears loyal and faithful to his father. Gloucester has been embarrassed about Edmund and has made him live abroad for the past nine years, but has now come to see his son differently. Gloucester's changes of mind and errors of judgement over his sons are shown later when he believes Edmund's lies about Edgar. Ironically, Gloucester only sees Edgar's true qualities after he is physically blind. By then, of course, the true Edgar is physically disguised as Tom O'Bedlam, seemingly identified with the forces of chaos, but in reality a symbol of injured innocence and loyalty. You should note that, though Edmund may have a grievance about his father's previous failure to recognise him, he is not deprived of his inheritance by Edgar's legitimacy. Edgar is not only legitimate, but also 'some year elder'.

Fathers and children

At the very start of the play this issue is raised, even before the dramatic scene where Lear gives all to his children. Gloucester's relationship to Edmund is ambiguous: he readily acknowledges him, but 'he hath been out nine years, and away he shall again.'

'Sir, I love you more than word can wield the matter; dearer than eye-sight, space and liberty'

Goneril's ironic words include the mention of eyesight – the first of many references to seeing and understanding. Later she and her accomplices will deprive others of their sight (the blinding of Gloucester), their space (usurping Lear's kingdom) and their liberty (imprisonment of Lear and Cordelia).

Blindness and
sight

'I am made of that self metal as my sister, And prize me at her worth.'

Regan emphasises the similarity between herself and her sister Goneril. The

two sisters often behave alike, although it is usually Goneril who takes the lead and who appears the stronger, more determined, ambitious and cruel of the two. It is Goneril, at the end of this scene, who suggests that Lear is now in his dotage and has become subject to the 'waywardness that infirm and choleric years bring with them' and that the sisters 'must do something, and i'th'heat'.

'Nothing will come of nothing: speak again.'

Lear is outraged at any sign of what he sees as disobedience, even from his

favourite daughter. The evidence of Lear's preference for Cordelia, doubtless formed in the days of his greater wisdom, is clear. He invites her to 'draw/A third more opulent' than her sisters. Since they have already been allocated their shares, his original plans must have included a favoured share for Cordelia.

King Lear

See what other examples you can find in this scene of comments which express his favouritism of his youngest daughter. Lear is unpredictable and violent, to the point of seeming irrational. The actions of Goneril and Regan are dictated by selfishness and cruelty. However, if you examine Lear's reaction to Cordelia's words, you may think that they have some justification in thinking him dangerously senile. In wanting to keep the prestige of being the monarch without carrying the associated responsibilities Lear makes a tragic mistake. His personality often seems to be as divided as his kingdom and his family. He seems unsure of his own self-image, and much of the play is concerned with issues of

18

self-realisation, personal identity and the search for an answer to his question: 'Who can tell me who I really am?' It is the asking of this question, and the answering of it, that surround Lear's madness.

Key scene

A crucial question in Act 1, Scene 1, is the state of Lear physically and mentally. In contrast to the uncertainty mentioned, look at the majesty and might of the speeches following Cordelia's refusal. Directors over the years have made very different decisions about how to present the King in this scene.

Cordelia

Cordelia's refusal to pander to her father's need for fawning and flattery initiates the main action of the play. Lear disowns her and turns to Goneril and Regan. On this level we can see Lear and Cordelia as two stubborn people who do in fact love each other, but who cannot back down once they have committed themselves to a position.

'Reserve thy state;
And in thy best consideration, check
This hideous rashness'

The Earl of Kent

Kent tries to persuade Lear against dividing his kingdom, especially as his daughters' flattering words have corrupted his judgement. Kent appears to realise what Lear seems to be blind to here; that he is so completely identified with his power and authority as king that he will be vulnerable once he has renounced his throne. Later we see how Lear is personally affected when he is no longer occupying the role of king: he has no authority and is cruelly treated.

Lear: 'Out of my sight!'
Kent: 'See better, Lear; and let me still remain
The true blank of thine eye.'

Kent tells Lear that he should reconsider his angry response and recognise that he is being given accurate (the central white 'blank' of a target in archery) and perceptive counsel. This scene abounds with references to seeing, eyes and eyesight. The implication of all these references is that Lear is deceived by appearances, whilst Kent and Cordelia are not.

'Hear me, recreant!
On thine allegiance, hear me!'

You should examine the speech banishing Kent in order to assess Lear's mental state at this time. He is very much a king: will the man who lays such stress on 'allegiance' and the impossibility of changing his mind be able to accept his own decision to give up power? Examine the speech for words and phrases that emphasise his position as absolute monarch. His decision is foolish, certainly, but he is in control of the situation, if not of himself. Look at the detailed arrangements he makes. Kent (apparently) obeys, delivering a rhyming couplet each to Lear, Cordelia, and Regan and Goneril. What impression do these couplets make on the audience?

'This is most strange,
That she, whom even but now was your best object...'

The King of France cannot understand why Lear should reject his favourite daughter, and indeed it is this which also convinces Goneril and Regan that their father's judgement has left him. It may be that Lear's obsessive devotion to Cordelia makes even her smallest faults too much for him to bear, although some critics have argued that Lear's obsession is not with love, but with control. He cannot bear others to be themselves and denies everyone this right, unless it conforms to his own expectations.

'Tis the infirmity of his age; yet he hath ever but slenderly known himself.'

Goneril and Regan are accurate observers of others. Here Regan's remarks sum up the play's central pivot – that Lear does not know what he really wants, or who he really is. Being king has meant that Lear has played a particular rôle in life, but when he gives this up he is forced to try to discover who he really is. The Fool and later Edgar, as Tom O'Bedlam, help him towards greater self-realisation by reminding him of his folly, forcing him to re-evaluate what it is to be a man.

Act 1 Scene 2

In the Earl of Gloucester's castle, his illegitimate son Edmund appears with a letter, supposedly from the Earl's legitimate son, Edgar. Edmund complains about the unfairness of his own illegitimate status and decides to use the letter to steal his brother's lands. When Gloucester arrives, Edmund pretends to hide the letter, which arouses Gloucester's curiosity so that he demands to read it. The letter suggests that Edmund should join Edgar in murdering their father. Edmund pretends that he thought the letter was a test of his love and says he will arrange for Gloucester to overhear a conversation between his two sons so that Gloucester can learn Edgar's true intentions. After Gloucester agrees and leaves, Edmund sneers at his father's foolish innocence. Edgar arrives and Edmund advises him to stay out of sight for a while and not to meet their father unless he is armed, for someone has made him furious with Edgar.

'Thou, nature, art my Goddess; to thy law My services are bound. '

Edmund complains that the traditional custom of the legitimate son inheriting the father's estate should not apply to him. By taking nature as his goddess, Edmund is explicitly rejecting the man-made laws of the state, describing them in terms of disease. He rejects the society which has rejected him. In this, Edmund stands opposed to the ideas of order and reason and alongside the forces of disruption in the play. By identifying Edmund with these 'modern' Renaissance ideas, Shakespeare is affirming the traditional values of the old order, represented by Lear, Kent, Edgar and Gloucester.

'Our father's love is to the bastard Edmund As to th'legitimate. Fine word, "legitimate"!'

Love

It is significant that Edmund's reason for wanting to unseat Edgar is purely materialistic. Despite what Edmund says, there is no evidence that his father loves him any the less. It seems clear that here the 'love' he refers to concerns the Earl's wealth rather than his affections; we saw at the start of the play that Gloucester was fulsome in his praise of Edmund and in no way ashamed to have him meet his friends. Little reason is given for Edmund's bitterness and he behaves throughout the play as the traditional male villain of contemporary drama.

In Shakespearean tragedy the characters likely to speak soliloquies are the heroes of the plays or villains who are carrying out devious plots. Thus, the audience can follow the thought processes and world-view of the heroes or, as here, enjoy the practice of villainy by sharing the villain's secrets. What do we learn of Edmund from this soliloquy? Look particularly at his language (with its continual emphasis on bastardy and legitimacy) and the argumentative, exclamatory style.

Fathers and children

Already the demands of paternal love have undermined the stability of the kingdom. Now the Gloucester sub-plot starts off with a statement of intent based upon the desire for inheritance: 'Legitimate Edgar, I must have your land.'

'Let's see: come, if it be nothing, I shall not need spectacles.'

The most ironic and poignant references to eyes and sight in the play come from Gloucester, who is deceived here by a false letter which Edmund shows him. Later, Gloucester learns through his suffering that whilst he had eyes he saw only

21

imperfectly. By the time of his death, however, he has indeed no need of spectacles.

'Nothing' is a constant motif of the play. You will be able to recall, for instance, that the turning-point of Act 1, Scene 1, was a dispute about 'nothing'.

'But I have heard him oft maintain…
… the father should be as ward to the son, and the son manage his revenue.'

Edmund

The illegitimate Edmund worms his way into Gloucester's thoughts by putting what are really his own words into the mouth of his absent brother Edgar. Edmund argues more openly later – along with Goneril and Regan – that the old become little more than a hindrance, a nuisance to be pushed out of the way by younger people. This impatient and domineering attitude is a warped reflection of Lear's own selfish fury, which comes back to haunt him. Edmund makes no concessions to filial love or respect. In his view, the lands and authority of the old should be confiscated and they should accept a back seat in their 'dotage'.

'… though the wisdom of nature can reason it thus and thus, yet nature finds itself scourg'd by the sequent effects.'

Order and reason

Gloucester argues that the moral and political chaos into which the state has fallen has been signalled by an equal disturbance in the order of the universe (eclipses, comets etc. were often seen at the time as portents of disaster). Edmund regards such thinking as 'the excellent foppery' (stupidity) 'of the world' and dismisses it scornfully. These two speeches repay careful reading, as they summarise very clearly both of the philosophies which are in conflict in the play and also highlight an important contemporary debate of Shakespeare's time.

Gloucester's argument rests on the assumption that there is a natural order and structure to which the universe must conform. His beliefs reflect his superstitious nature and his naivety; an unreflective trait also seen in the way he quickly accepts Edmund's lies about Edgar. The contrast between this feeble, old man and Kent is repeatedly placed before the audience.

It was commonly believed at the time that the actions of humankind, especially those affecting the great and powerful, brought about heavenly expressions of judgement. Thus, Lear's dismembered kingdom produces a civil strife which is echoed both in the tempests of the skies and those in his mind. Edmund, however, feels that his advancement in the world is due solely to his own ability and intelligence and is therefore fully deserved, owing nothing to any divine master-plan.

'I promise you the effects he writes of succeed unhappily...'

Edgar and Edmund discuss the omens signalled by recent astronomical events. Edmund, who has just mocked such superstitions to Gloucester, not only now suggests to Edgar that relationships do exist between events in the heavens and those on earth, but then goes on to list precisely the kinds of calamity which actually befall characters in the play. Once again, we see Edmund showing a false face to the world.

Blindness and sight

The contrast between appearance and reality is stressed in the references throughout the play to blindness and sight. Edmund appears always as himself but is never what he seems to be, whilst Edgar appears as himself only rarely and spends most of the play concealing his goodness from the evils of the world in the guise of Tom O'Bedlam.

Edmund is given a soliloquy at each stage of this first deception. The opening 22 lines express his philosophy of life; the prose soliloquy in the middle shows contempt for his father and brother and explains his change of role; the final six lines sum up the progress he is making and the reasons for his success. Notice that he is able to deceive Edgar because of the latter's good qualities, not his failings, though it is Gloucester's 'credulous' nature that makes him an easy victim.

Act 1 Scene 3

In the Duke of Albany's palace, Goneril complains about the behaviour of her father's knights and his criticisms of her. She tells her servant Oswald to instruct everyone to be unkind and offhand to Lear and his knights from now on.

'Put on what weary negligence you please, You and your fellows'

Goneril deliberately orders Oswald to behave in a way which she knows will

Goneril and Regan

provoke Lear's anger. She has no hesitation in confronting Lear and later unflinchingly takes the brunt of his anger and his violent curses. Notice that Goneril does not seek her husband's advice here: throughout the first three acts of the play she dominates him and later turns on him viciously, when he criticises her for her actions. Regan, on the other hand, tends to follow her husband to a much greater extent.

Act 1 Scene 4

The banished Kent arrives in disguise at Lear's court in the Duke of Albany's palace and is accepted into service by him. When Oswald, the servant, is disrespectful to Lear, Kent trips him up and rebukes him, then drives him out. The Fool mocks Lear for giving away his kingdom. Goneril arrives, angry at the behaviour of her father's knights and, to Lear's astonishment, criticises him for this. Lear declares that he will not stay to hear further ingratitude, but will go to Regan's castle. Goneril insists that her father's force of a hundred knights is a threat which must be reduced. Goneril's husband Albany thinks her behaviour is too harsh, but she overrules him and sends a letter with Oswald to Regan, in which she communicates her feelings about their father and his knights.

'I do profess to be no less than I seem'

Kent returns in disguise to serve Lear. Notice the clever irony in what he says here: he is no less than he may appear to be, but he is certainly more than meets the eye. There is also another irony at work here. Kent sometimes goes to great lengths to speak the truth bluntly, through most of the play he successfully maintains a disguise that deceives even those who know him well. Kent's disguise is no more than that – a device behind which he conceals himself – and it serves no other purpose. But the pretended madness of Edgar is not just a disguise for self-protection, it is a dramatic device to represent a particular view of humanity.

'Dost thou know me, fellow?'

Lear asks Kent if he recognises him. Ironically, it is Lear who does not know Kent: the implication is that Lear does not know himself, either. In contrast to Kent's comment that Lear carries authority in his face and bearing, the servants treat Lear as though he is of no importance. The Fool characteristically criticises Lear for his foolishness in giving away all his authority to become 'an O without a figure.'

Blindness and
sight

'Since my young Lady's going into France, Sir, the Fool hath much pined away.'

Although Cordelia is absent for much of the play, touches like this one serve to remind us continually of her effect on her father. He will have 'no more of that' when the knight reminds him of the Fool's sadness at Cordelia's rejection. Lear turns away from the memory of Cordelia's refusal to obey him, like one who flinches from a fresh wound. Though the two never appear together there is some sort of a link established between Cordelia and the Fool: at the very end, which one of them is the 'poor fool' who is hanged? Here the Fool's pining for Cordelia serves to reveal Lear's sensitivity to an unwelcome truth.

Cordelia

'...they'll have me whipp'd for speaking true, thou'lt have me whipped for lying'

The Fool's witty comment here is more than just an insight into the

The Fool

unpredictability of Lear's temper. It acts as one of the many observations which are sharp enough to hurt the king. Examine the Fool's rhymes and riddles in this scene (from offering Kent his cap to the entry of Goneril) and work out the various supposedly comic ways in which he comments bitterly on Lear's folly and his powerlessness. Lear's threats to have him whipped remind us of the fate of other characters (Kent, Cordelia) who express love and loyalty through honesty.

'Not only, sir, this your all-licens'd fool...'

Goneril and Regan

Goneril has some justice on her side. She later describes the knights as 'so disorder'd, so debosh'd (debauched) and bold/That this our court.../Shows like a riotous inn.' This is, no doubt, an exaggeration, but with a strong element of truth. What, then, is so offensive about her speech? Look at words like 'insolent', 'not-to-be-endured', 'censure' and 'redress'. Who do you think is now the authority figure? In her second speech her disgust with the knights (and, therefore, her father) is evident in her choice of words.

Lear: 'Who is it that can tell me who I am?'
The Fool: 'Lear's shadow.'

King Lear

If Lear's existence is defined in terms of his military might and authority, then without his throne and his power he ceases to exist; hence the Fool's reply here. This scene reaches a climax with Goneril's demand that Lear reduce the number of his knights and Lear's inflamed reaction to this. See what earlier examples you can find of seemingly small incidents that show lack of respect for Lear.

On a more general level, notice the large number of occasions in the play where characters ask others who they are, or ask how others come to know (recognise/understand) them. These questions express, on a simple level, humankind's deeper and constant search for self-knowledge.

'Hear, Nature, hear! dear goddess, hear!'

Lear finds it almost impossible to show any feeling except anger in the first two acts of the play. He needs absolute obedience and, when deprived of it, explodes in a fury that has more than a hint of his future madness. Like Edmund, he calls on Nature as his goddess: the pagan beliefs of Ancient Britain are frequently hinted at in the play, though the court, titles, etc., clearly suggest a later age.

Fathers and children

As Lear realises that he has made a terrible mistake, he curses Goneril in terms that emphasise children, childbirth and sterility. The final statement of parental suffering is especially memorable: 'How sharper than a serpent's tooth it is/To have a thankless child!'

Lear's great curse destroys any hint of love of family, with its emphasis on sterility and the destructive effects of disloyalty in children. Lear's revenge on Goneril will come if she has to share the pain of 'a thankless child'. How aware do you think Lear is of the true situation at this stage? 'Woe, that too late repents', he says, which implies awareness of his error; what do we learn from his comments about Cordelia and Regan?

Lear is also made angry by his own reaction. While Goneril remains infuriatingly in control of herself and Albany fails to make any impact, Lear weeps. In his shame at this, he threatens to pluck out his own eyes in an anticipation of the later blinding of Gloucester.

Blindness and sight

Act 1 Scene 5

From the Duke of Albany's palace, Lear sends his new servant (Kent in disguise) with letters to Regan's husband, the Earl of Gloucester. As they make ready to leave, the Fool continues to ridicule Lear for his lack of wisdom.

'O! Let me not be mad, not mad, sweet heaven; Keep me in temper; I would not be mad!'

Lear's comments here are the first sign of what is to come. He says he will forget his 'nature', meaning his kindness as a father, but we might ask what Lear's real nature is – another matter which soon comes to preoccupy him, although he never really indulges in careful self-examination.

Madness

Lear's progress towards madness is well-charted, though its actual starting-point may be debated. Here he fears it as a consequence; by Act 2, Scene 4 it is imminent ('do not make me mad' and 'I shall go mad'); in Act 3, Scene 2 he realises 'my wits begin to turn'.

Self-test Questions Act 1

Uncover the plot
Delete two of the three alternatives given, to find the correct plot. Beware possible misconceptions and muddles.

Two of King Lear's daughters are married: Regan/Goneril/Cordelia to the Duke of Albany; Goneril/Regan/Cordelia to the Duke of Cornwall. The King of France and the Duke of Burgundy both seek to marry Cordelia/Goneril/Regan. Goneril/Regan/Cordelia and Goneril/Cordelia/Regan tell Lear they love him more than anything else, but Goneril/Rosalind/Cordelia refuses. Lear becomes furious and disowns Cordelia/Goneril/Regan. Albany/Kent/Edmund, who argues against this, is imprisoned/blinded/banished. Burgundy/France/Albany refuses to accept Goneril/Juliet/Cordelia, but Burgundy/France/Albany does and they go off to Burgundy/Dover/France together. Goneril/Regan/Desdemona and Goneril/Regan/Celia say they will deal with Lear because he has become insane/infirm/angry and troublesome. The Earl of Gloucester's illegitimate son Edgar/Edmund/Oswald has a hidden locket/secret parcel/forged letter. He says he will use this to have his brother killed/steal his brother's lands/blackmail the Earl. It contains plans about kidnapping/murdering/blinding Gloucester. Edmund/Edgar/Gloucester tells Burgundy/Edgar/Gloucester to hide. Goneril/Regan/Cordelia ensures that her servants are attentive/rude/violent to Lear and his knights. Albany/Kent/Edmund successfully gets back into Lear's court because he is disguised/forgiven/punished. Goneril/Regan/Cordelia becomes angry at the behaviour of Lear's knights/Fool/servants. Lear says he will punish them/ignore her/leave. Albany is relieved/unhappy/glad about this. Meanwhile, the Fool ridicules/consoles/attacks Lear for his lack of land/wisdom/money.

Who? What? Why? When? Where? How?
1   How old does Kent say he is?
2   What reason does Goneril give Albany for wanting to cut down the number of Lear's knights?
3   To whom does Lear write a letter?
4   What answer does Lear receive to his question; 'Who is it that can tell me who I am'?
5   Who is told to put on 'weary negligence' towards whom, and by whom?
6   According to Goneril's first opinion, how many knights should Lear have?
7   How does Kent behave towards Oswald, and why?
8   Who is punished for telling the truth and also for telling lies, and by whom?
9   Which two crowns does the Fool offer to give Lear?
10 What reason does Kent give for returning to court after his banishment?

Who said that, and to whom?
1   'I love you more than word can wield the matter.'
2   'Fairest …, that art most rich, being poor:'
3   'I shall not need spectacles.'
4   'Who is it that can tell me who I am?'
5   'Reserve thy state.'
6   'Some villain hath done me wrong.'
7   'Nothing will come of nothing.'
8   'I do profess to be no less than I seem.'
9   'Thou, Nature, art my goddess.'
10 'Meantime we shall express our darker purpose.'

Open quotes
Identify the scene; complete the phrase; identify the speaker and the character being spoken to.
1 'The quality of nothing hath not such need to hide itself. Let's see: come,'
2 'All thy other titles thou hast given away;'
3 ''Tis the infirmity of his age;'
4 'The hedge-sparrow fed the cuckoo so long,'
5 'How sharper than a serpent's tooth it is...'
6 'Ingratitude, thou marble-hearted fiend,/More hideous, when...'
7 'I am made of that self metal...'
8 'This is the excellent foppery of the world, that, when we are sick in fortune,...'
9 'they'll have me whipp'd for...'
10 'Fare thee well, King; sith thus thou wilt appear,'

Act 2 Scene 1

News arrives at the Earl of Gloucester's castle that Regan and her husband the Duke of Cornwall will soon be arriving. The courtier Curan tells Edmund of the rumours of wars between Cornwall and Albany. When Edgar appears, Edmund tells him he must flee for his life. Edmund says he will help him by pretending to have a sword fight with him so that Edgar may escape in the confusion. After wounding himself, Edmund tells Gloucester that Edgar attacked him when he would not agree to join a plot to kill their father. Gloucester says he will have Edgar arrested and killed, then make Edmund his legitimate heir. Cornwall and Regan arrive and praise Edmund for his actions, taking him into their service.

'Persuade me to the murder of your lordship'

Edgar and Gloucester are, of course, very trusting victims of Edmund: they

never question his honesty or advice. However, you should take note equally of the conviction that Edmund brings to his deception. The intensity and the willingness to wound himself to fake evidence help to convince, and the vocabulary of his speeches to Gloucester is perfect to impress an old man who fears that the old standards are disappearing. Find examples of diction that emphasise evil, unnatural actions and, on the other hand, right and principle.

'The noble Duke my master, My worthy arch and patron, comes to-night'

Gloucester is mistaken on all counts here: Cornwall is neither noble nor friend to him; his orders for the capture of his son Edgar are aimed at the wrong son; and his unquestioning belief in the loyalty of others is consistently faulty. Only later in the play does Gloucester's suffering allow him to understand the world better. This lack of perception extends even to a surprising absence of any suspicion when, later, Regan somehow appears to know at once why Gloucester's 'heart is crack'd'.

Act 2 Scene 2

Outside Gloucester's castle, Kent roundly insults and beats Oswald. Edmund, Cornwall, Regan and Gloucester appear and in answer to Cornwall's questions, Kent says he administered the beating because Oswald is a rogue and a scoundrel. Oswald denies this, saying that Kent beat him because this pleased Lear. Cornwall has Kent put in the stocks, even though Kent tells him that he is the king's messenger. Gloucester tries to intervene, but to no avail. When Kent is left alone, he begins to read a letter from Cordelia, who has heard about his banishment. He then falls asleep.

'A knave, a rascal, an eater of broken meats...'

In response to Oswald's question 'What dost thou know me for?' Kent launches into a sustained outpouring of abuse which is often very funny when played in the theatre – the more so because most audiences will think it well-deserved and well-aimed. Kent's eloquent and rather startling tongue-lashing also shows us that he is not always a man of few words. Kent's language derives from his contempt for Oswald and his natural bluntness, but also from the fact that he is in disguise. Shakespeare very convincingly uses more extreme speech patterns when a character is assuming a role: either a different person (Kent; Edgar) or a disguised character (Edmund; Goneril and Regan in the first scene). Here Kent, as the servant Caius, typically expresses his fury in compound descriptions: 'lily-livered', 'glass-gazing', 'one-trunk-inheriting', etc. Later he over-plays the role of the blunt servant by ignoring the Duke of Cornwall to continue his tirade: is this role-playing or is it genuine fury?

'Sir, in good faith, in sincere verity, Under th'allowance of your great aspect'

Kent deliberately mocks the ornate, courtly style of language which he associates with scoundrels like Oswald. This speech also contrasts with the blunt abuse which he has just hurled at the servant. But Kent seems to be quite unnecessarily provocative, and it comes as no real surprise that Cornwall puts him in the stocks. We might recall Cordelia's behaviour at the start of the play and wonder whether she was right to think that sometimes it may be better to remain silent.

'Fortune, good night; smile once more; turn thy wheel!'

Kent sits in the stocks and considers the turning of fortune's wheel, and life's ups and downs. Whilst his suffering is not on the same scale as, say, Gloucester's blinding or Lear's rejection by Goneril and Regan, Kent's good-humoured attitude to being put in the stocks emphasises one of the play's moral arguments – that humankind should accept its fate, not fight against it.

The turning of fortune's wheel was a popular contemporary metaphor, reflecting a widely (but not universally) held view of the nature of the universe. Other examples abound in the play: Lear is reduced to a semi-naked wretch wandering across the darkened heath in the middle of a storm; and Gloucester's noble and honest son Edgar becomes Tom O'Bedlam.

The suffering and tragedy which befall some characters in the play are shown to be brought about by their refusal to accept their fate. Examples include Lear's unwillingness to shoulder the proper responsibilities of a monarch; Cordelia's refusal to give proper due to a father's expectations about the obedience of his children; Edmund's resentment of his illegitimate status; and Goneril and Regan's ill-treatment of their father.

Act 2 Scene 3

Edgar, who is hiding in a wood, has heard that he is a wanted man. He has escaped from the search party and decides that for his own safety he will disguise himself as Tom, a wandering madman from Bedlam.

In this short scene of some 20 lines, Edgar announces to the audience that he

Edgar

is going to act a part. Unlike Lear, he will only pretend to be mad. Contrast this disguise with that of Kent, who replaces himself with another interpretation of the same values and behaviour. Kent's disguise will allow him to carry on doing what he did before – serve his master. Edgar's disguise, instead, has to perform a particular function. It will enable others, and perhaps him also, to understand themselves more.

Madness

In contrast to Lear's slide into madness, Edgar here carries out a transformation scene. Beginning with the reason for disguise ('I heard myself proclaim'd'), he takes on the part of Tom as he changes his outward appearance and his speech. By the end of the scene he is crying out as poor Tom and Edgar no longer

---

Act 2 Scene 4

Lear arrives outside Gloucester's castle and finds Kent in the stocks. Kent explains how this came about and the Fool mocks him for wanting to serve a master whose power is

in decline. Lear is furious when Regan and Cornwall at first send messages that they are too tired and ill to see him. They eventually appear and Kent is freed from the stocks. When Lear tells Regan how her sister has treated him, she advises him to apologise to Goneril and mend their disagreements. Goneril arrives and Regan sides with her in saying that Lear should dismiss his men, after which he may come to stay with her. Lear is furious at the way they are both treating him and rages out into the developing storm. Gloucester pleads with Goneril and Regan to house their father and his men, but both they and Cornwall argue that Lear has brought things on himself and must suffer for his own foolishness.

'They durst not do't,
They could not, would not do't; 'tis worse than murther,'

Love

This section, where Lear cannot believe that his daughters have put Kent in the stocks, underlines how divorced from reality the king has been. He has been a man with no understanding of his own or other people's feelings. We saw this at the start of the play when he assumed that his demand for a show of affection from his daughters would produce real feelings of love. Lear's treatment of Cordelia at the start of the play seems harsh only if we assume that he understands love. Lear seems not to feel any affection or love, only to demand it. Yet he has a great need to be loved, as he finally recognises towards the end of the play.

'Let go thy hold when a great wheel
runs down a hill, lest it break thy neck with following…'

The Fool

The Fool often speaks wisely when others speak or behave foolishly, as here when he advises Kent about attaching his fate to that of another. The Fool's wit is always applied with a purpose, and like the later madness of Lear, often contains perceptive insights into reality. Significantly, it is not until Lear becomes mad that he starts to reflect upon the ways of the world; he has never been a thoughtful man before.

'Deny to speak with me? They are sick? They are weary?
They have travell'd all the night? …
Fetch me a better answer.'

Goneril and Regan

Unlike Goneril in Act 1, who stood up to Lear's curses face to face and did not flinch, Regan tries to avoid meeting her father and makes excuses instead. Once summoned out in no uncertain terms, she comes at once, but then tries to make excuses why she cannot accommodate all her father's knights. However, although less aggressive than Goneril, Regan is equally unyielding. All her speeches of any length make the point that

Goneril has done nothing wrong and Lear should return to her. When Goneril arrives, Regan allies with her in a direct confrontation with Lear. Though Regan appears gentler than Goneril (a fond belief that Lear clings to desperately), it is she who first proposes a reduction to 25 knights and who clinches the appalling reverse auction by the simple question, 'What need one?'.

Key scene

The cold calculations of the two sisters and Lear's awareness of helplessness, leading to flight, provide one of the great turning points of the play. Goneril and Regan appear to be speaking in all reasonableness until discussion of generalisations suddenly becomes a rapid reduction of numbers.

Although the sisters are in many ways alike, their relationship seems brittle and unfounded upon anything except their joint purpose in seeking power and we should not be surprised when they eventually turn on each other in mutual suspicion and jealousy.

Lear: 'I gave you all –'
Regan: 'And in good time you gave it.'

Order and reason

Regan expresses the same ungrateful, sneering feelings towards Lear which Edmund has for Gloucester. Both reject not only the call of honour and obedience but also turn their backs on the possibility of love and its ability to redeem and transform. Lear's failure to understand love continues, with his pathetic belief that Goneril has 'twice her love' because at that stage she seems to be allowing twice the number of knights.

'O! Reason not the need; our basest beggars
Are in the poorest thing superfluous'

Blindness and sight

Now that Lear realises what it will mean to be without the power of his knights, he begins to understand that a person's real needs encompass more than just what is necessary for mere survival. This increased awareness marks a change from his behaviour when he criticised Cordelia for refusing to mouth platitudes of love like her sisters. Lear has started to understand something about himself which will eventually enable him to gain more insight into the character of others. This speech echoes Lear's descent into madness, beginning as it does with a powerful defence of the dignity of humankind and then degenerating into incoherence.

Key scene/Madness

Equally as important as Goneril and Regan allying against their father is his reaction. He has many choices other than fleeing to destinations unknown, and the way that broken exclamations follow the reasoned fury of the speech's opening marks Lear's descent into madness.

Lear's cries here also reintroduce the importance of materialism as another of

Love

the play's themes. Lear is variously defined by the kingdom he has power over, the children who must speak only what he wishes to hear, the nobles who must obey his every whim and the knights who make up his train of followers. As Edgar comes to recognise later on, by himself he is nothing. It is this belief that someone is no more than the things they own or control which drives Edmund, Goneril and Regan. Only when Lear begins to see through these surface impressions does he come to learn anything of himself or to appreciate the open, simple honesty of Cordelia's love.

'You think I'll weep; No, I'll not weep'

When Lear discovers that both Goneril and Regan are determined to remove

King Lear

his knights and, as he sees it, reduce him to 'a poor old man' he says he will not weep, although he has good cause. He rages at the way he has been treated and feels betrayed by his ungrateful 'pelican' daughters. Throughout the first two acts we see that Lear seems to deal with the world only through anger. Here he makes it clear that his fury will drive him either to tears or madness. We see from what follows that Lear cannot yet face a world which is full of feelings and so chooses madness.

'The injuries that they themselves procure Must be their schoolmasters.'

Whatever else Regan may be, here she shows herself to be an accurate judge of character, for Lear does indeed bring much of his trouble upon himself.

Goneril and Regan

Goneril and Regan function almost as agents of divine will, punishing Lear for his sins. They are not without good qualities; Goneril has courage and strength of will, for example. But their evil lies in the misapplication of their qualities of character; their refusal to accept the proper functioning of the family and the state marks them as agents of disorder.

▪ Self-test questions Act 2

Uncover the plot
Delete two of the three alternatives given, to find the correct plot. Beware possible misconceptions and muddles.

Edmund/Lear/Albany tells the Fool/Edgar/Albany that he must run away, and fakes a letter/fire/sword fight to help him escape. After wounding/hiding/blinding himself, Edmund/the Fool/Albany tells Gloucester/Cornwall/Lear that Banquo/Edgar/Albany attacked him because he would not agree to join a murder/kidnap /traitorous plot. Gloucester/Cornwall/Macbeth says Romeo/Edgar/Albany is to be rewarded/banished/killed and Edmund/Malvolio/Albany will be his legitimate heir. Cornwall takes Tom/Burgundy/Edmund into his service. Lear/Gloucester/Kent beats Oswald/Edmund/the Fool for being a rogue and a scoundrel and France/Cornwall/Albany has him put in the stocks for this. Edmund/Lear/Edgar decides to disguise himself. He will be Bedlam/Tom/Curan, a wandering beggar/player/ madman. Lear/Gloucester/Kent is angry to see Macbeth/Malvolio/Kent in the stocks, and when Goneril/Regan/Cordelia and Albany/Burgundy/Cornwall at first say they will not see him. They say they are too angry/tired/bored and ill/busy /indifferent. Juliet/Regan/Cordelia says Lear should return to Goneril/Ophelia/ Desdemona. Goneril/Regan/Juliet says, with Bianca/Regan/Cordelia, that Lear should dismiss his Fool/servants/men. Lear is furious and leaves even though he does not want to/he does not know where he will go/a storm is developing. Gloucester/Kent/Albany pleads with Goneril/Regan/Ophelia and Goneril/Regan/ Juliet to house Lear and his men but they and Edmund/Cornwall/Oswald say that Lear must suffer for his own foolishness.

Who? What? Why? When? Where? How?
1   Who is whose 'worthy arch and patron'?
2   Where does Edgar say he hid to escape being captured?
3   How many followers does Lear bring to Gloucester's castle?
4   How does Kent pass the time in the stocks?
5   Who argues against Kent being put in the stocks and why?
6   Who interrupts Kent's beating of Oswald?
7   What reason does Regan give for coming to Gloucester's castle?
8   According to Kent, how long is it since he last met Oswald?
9   How does Lear at first respond to Regan's suggestion that he return to Goneril and apologise?
10 How does Edmund give more credibility to his account of being attacked?

Who said that, and to whom?
1   'Natures of such deep trust we shall much need.'
2   'Such smiling rogues as these,/Like rats, oft bite the holy cords a-twain...'
3   '...thou shalt never have my curse...'
4   ''Tis best to give him way; he leads himself.'
5   'I have full cause of weeping.'
6   '...our basest beggars/Are in the poorest thing superfluous.'
7   'In cunning I must draw my sword upon you.'
8   'I am too old to learn.'
9   'Fetch me a better answer.'
10 'Why, what a monstrous fellow art thou.'

Open quotes
Identify the scene; complete the phrase; identify the speaker and the character being spoken to.
1 "'tis the Duke's pleasure,/Whose disposition, all the world well knows,…'
2 'O! Sir, to wilful men,/The injuries that they themselves procure…'
3 'Dear daughter, I confess that I am old;…'
4 'This is some fellow,/Who, having been prais'd for bluntness,…'
5 'O, Sir! You are old;/Nature in you…'
6 'Poor Turlygood! Poor Tom! That's…'
7 'I will tread this unbolted villain into mortar,'
8 'Where may we set our horses?'
9 'I have seen better faces in my time…'
10 'Let go thy hold when a great wheel runs down a hill,…'

Act 3 Scene 1

Kent and a gentleman meet upon a heath in the storm. Kent learns that Lear is raging in the storm, attended only by his Fool. Kent gives the gentleman a ring which will identify him to Cordelia and tells him to report the situation to her in Dover, where she has arrived with an army.

'Contending with the fretful elements; Bids the wind blow the earth into the sea'

The gentleman tells Kent of Lear's raging. Lear's self-centredness and childish

petulance is self-destructive, but because he cannot get his own way he has turned his fury upon the world, which he wants to destroy because it will not do as he wishes. Lear's fury is also directed at the way he has been betrayed, although you may feel that this is also due to his previous willingness to base

Order and reason

his judgement of character on surface appearances.

Act 3 Scene 2

Lear rages on the heath at the surrounding storm as the Fool tries to get him to shelter. Kent appears and persuades Lear to seek out a nearby hovel.

'Blow, winds, and crack your cheeks! Rage! Blow!'

Throughout the first part of the play we see Lear increasingly in the grip of

a terrible rage. This culminates in the storm around which the action of the play revolves, for the first half of the play leads up to it and the second half deals with the effects it has wrought on Lear. Nowhere else in the play is Lear's fury seen to the same degree as here. On the heath, before being

King Lear

persuaded into the hovel, Lear has three great speeches

Blindness and sight

challenging the storm, not particularly long (about 10 lines each), but immensely powerful, with a crazed majesty. See if you can identify the differences between them. The first invites destruction, and the diction reflects this destruction and the might of Nature: 'all-shaking thunder', 'cataracts and hurricanes', 'oak-cleaving thunderbolts', etc. The last words hint that 'ingrateful man' deserves this. In the other two speeches ('Rumble thy bellyful! ...' and 'Let the great gods...') the sins of Mankind are more fully developed: make a note of Lear's accusations against humanity and how he sees himself in the scale of human sin and suffering.

Key scene

The storm scenes are important for many reasons, but the remarkable quality of the language is one of the major reasons. Remember that Shakespeare did not have available the range of stage effects we have today. This astonishing outburst of language is a more than satisfactory substitute.

Later in the play, the doctor observes that only when Lear's rage has passed will he stand any chance of recovery – but that by then, his fury will have done him permanent harm. After his madness passes, Lear begins to see the world more as it is and less the way he had imagined; he sees Goneril and Regan for what they are; believes that Cordelia loves him; accepts Kent's service and is more understanding towards others, even feeling pity for the Fool and the 'poor naked wretches' of his kingdom.

Madness

Oddly in Lear madness and insight develop together. As he realises 'my wits begin to turn' and challenges the storm in magnificent absurdity, he also begins to understand the hidden guilt and the sufferings of Mankind.

'My wits begin to turn.
Come on, my boy. How dost, my boy? Art cold?'

After Lear's raging he begins to show some sensitivity towards others, as here

Love

when he tells the Fool and Kent to seek shelter ahead of him from the storm and driving rain – unusual behaviour for even the most kindly king. This type of behaviour marks the beginning of Lear's self-awareness, as opposed to his self-pity. Throughout the king's journey towards greater self-knowledge, the Fool performs an important function in helping Lear to discover a new vision of the world around him, often by reflecting Lear not as he likes to think of himself, but as he really is.

Act 3 Scene 3

In a room in his castle, Gloucester tells Edmund that Cornwall, as his superior, has commandeered the castle and forbidden him to show Lear any hospitality. He also tells Edmund that he has received a secret letter which contains news that a military power is preparing itself to revenge Lear for the way he has been treated. When Gloucester leaves, Edmund decides to betray his father so that he will get all his possessions and land.

'The younger rises when the old doth fall'

In a brief scene filled with irony, Gloucester innocently confesses his fears and secrets to the one person who most seeks to destroy him, whilst Edmund speaks what could be his own eulogy.

Act 3 Scene 4

Outside the hovel on the heath, Lear tells Kent that he feels little of the surrounding tempest because of the mental torment he is suffering. He thinks about the poor and homeless and realises that he gave such people no thought when he ruled as king. He sends the Fool into the hovel, inside which is Edgar (disguised as Tom O' Bedlam) raving about how he is tormented by devils. Edgar says he is being punished for sleeping with his mistress and for a host of other base sins. Gloucester arrives to offer them all shelter, even though he has been forbidden to do so, and says that Goneril and Regan want their father dead.

'Poor naked wretches, whereso'er you are
That bide the pelting of this pitiless storm'

During Lear's wanderings – literally a journey into self-discovery – he comes to appreciate that he has been wilfully ignorant of the world around him. He pities the homeless, the hungry and the ragged and says he will expose himself to what they experience. He wishes to do something about his ignorance of the reality of life as experienced by his subjects.

Blindness and sight

'Bless thy five wits! Tom's a-cold. O! Do de, do de, do de.'

When behaving as Tom O'Bedlam, Edgar speaks in an unnatural way. Tom's

meaning is often almost impenetrable and his rantings make Lear sound sensible. Tom's ranting, like the raving of Lear and the verbal juggling of the Fool, forms almost another language within the play – another expression of the reality of the world for these characters, of which only they seem able to make any sense. It is within this bizarre context that the mock

Edgar

trial of Goneril and Regan takes place.

Madness/Key scene

It is important to realise that the unique power of the central section of the play comes from creating a world where madness is the norm, with its own crazed logic. 'Tom' is now the philosopher and the representative of the world outside, Gloucester, is identified with 'the foul fiend Flibbertigibbet'.

The apparent gibberish of the Fool, Lear and Tom O'Bedlam has a subtler function within the play than merely the depiction of various states of mind

– whether deranged, feigned or otherwise. The language of these three characters is linked to the play's exploration of how things seem to be, as compared to how they really are. It is another expression of what it really means to understand, or 'see', the world clearly and what it means to be blind to it. Tom, Lear and the Fool often make quite startling sense inside what at first seems like nonsense.

'Death, traitor! Nothing could have subdu'd nature To such a lowness but his unkind daughters.'

Lear blames his daughters for all that has befallen him, rather than his own lack of judgement for bringing his problems upon himself. He sees all men's punishments as a result of having daughters. In a sense Lear is right, for his daughters, as a reflection of himself, are a part of him and he is being destroyed by weapons of his own creation.

'This cold night will turn us all to fools and madmen.'

Surrounded as he seems to be by the ravings of lunatics, the Fool shows the audience the face of sanity. As if to underline the way Lear's madness is increasing, we find his use of language, both here and in the 'trial' scene, coming ever closer to that of the Fool.

'A servingman, proud in heart and mind; that curl'd my hair, wore gloves in my cap...'

Edgar replies to Lear's question 'What hast thou been?' with a list which

echoes in many ways the long string of abuses which Kent flings in the face of Oswald in Act 2, scene 2. In both, humankind is described as lecherous, base and superficial, with frequent references to unpleasant animal images. Unlike Kent's attack on Oswald, which is largely a stream of amusing invective, this speech of Edgar's is more measured, stately and poetic, before subsiding into nonsense jingles. This is appropriate because whilst Kent is haranguing a rogue, Lear and Edgar are actually debating the essence of the human condition.

'Is man no more than this? Consider him well.'

Lear sees Tom O'Bedlam as representing the real nature of humankind: a

'poor, bare, forked animal', whom he will join by tearing off his own clothing and standing naked under the storm's fury. Lear has yet to realise that it is his relationship with the world around him, and especially with those who love and serve him and to whom he is indebted, which defines who he is. He has begun to see that as a lonely individual, he is nothing. The

Love

real response to Lear's question is signalled by the re-entry of Gloucester who, significantly, bears a light to guide Lear to shelter and warmth.

'Poor Tom; that eats the swimming frog, the toad, the tadpole, the wall-newt, and the water'

Lear sees Tom O'Bedlam as an 'unaccommodated man'. Tom's own

description here accords well with Lear's view. Just as Lear has fallen from kingship to wandering madman, so Edgar – who once was to inherit an earldom – now covers himself in dirt, wears nothing but a blanket and lives in a hovel. Although Edgar's madness is merely a disguise, his physical deprivation

Edgar

is real and his transformation in the play is an example of how fortune's great wheel turns for everyone.

Tom O'Bedlam stands for what humanity is at base, when deprived of the surface trappings of civilisation. He is an example to Lear of the universal chaos which lies in wait for him also, if he will not accept his proper destiny and be

Order and
reason

reconciled into God's ordered universe.

'First let me talk with this philosopher. What is the cause of thunder?'

It is significant that Lear is given no answer to this question. Shakespeare's

subtle use of character throughout the play is well illustrated here. At one level, Lear is seeking to understand something of the nature of the world around him and asks the madman Tom O' Bedlam to help him. Lear is mad, but seems not to regard himself as such. He sees Tom O' Bedlam as a scholarly

King Lear

philosopher from whom he may learn something of the truth about the world. But Tom O' Bedlam is really Edgar, who only pretends to be mad for his own safety and can indeed teach Lear something about betrayal, loyalty and the reading of the character of others.

Lear is also seeking to understand the storm within himself, of which the larger turmoil in nature is both a metaphor and a parody. It is ironic that Lear searches for order and reason around and within him in a conversation between a madman, a feigned madman, a Fool and a friend in disguise.

'Ah! that good Kent...'

Gloucester's speech to the disguised Kent is full of irony. He speaks of Kent and the son 'now outlaw'd', in the total unawareness of their presence. Twice he aligns himself with Lear (and, of course, 'poor Tom') in seeing madness creeping up on him. Gloucester, metaphorically blind, soon to be literally so, is redeemed by the sympathy he feels for the outcasts (whom he is soon to join) and by his willingness to admit his love for Edgar, even when he has no doubt of his guilt.

Act 3 Scene 5

In a room in Gloucester's castle, Cornwall learns of Gloucester's letter from Edmund. Cornwall tells Edmund that he will now become Earl of Gloucester and sends him off to arrest his father.

'This is the letter he spoke of, which approves him an intelligent party to the advantages of France.'

Edmund lies to and cheats everyone he meets, without exception. For the second time he uses a letter to betray those for whom he should feel the greatest love and to whom he should owe the greatest loyalty: first his brother, now his father. It does not matter to Edmund, as Cornwall seems to sense; 'True or false, it hath made thee Earl of Gloucester'.

Act 3 Scene 6

Gloucester leaves Kent, Lear, Edgar and the Fool in a warm room, where Lear conducts a mock-trial of Goneril and Regan. Gloucester returns and tells them all to flee to Dover, for their lives are threatened. Kent and the Fool carry off Lear on a litter. Left alone, Edgar decides that his own troubles seem bearable now that he has seen those which others suffer.

'It shall be done; I will arraign them straight. Come, sit thou here, most learned justicer'

Lear conducts a mock-trial of Goneril and Regan, with Tom O' Bedlam (Edgar) as his assistant judge. Although it contains elements of the bizarre and surreal, the mock-trial indicates that a desire for order and justice is starting to replace the chaos and thoughts of savage revenge in Lear's mind. As such, it marks the start of his journey away from insanity.

Order and reason

Madness

As Lear attempts to impose some form of order, he collapses into confusion and sleep. He can set up the court, but he cannot remember the evidence. The accusation that Goneril 'kicked the poor king her father' is a jumbled recollection of various events, including Kent and Oswald.

The characters involved in the trial represent the elements in the struggle in Lear's kingdom between order and reason against madness, blindness against sight. Lear, who is mad because of his earlier blindness, now sits in judgement on a joint-stool. This represents Goneril to him, for in his world nothing is now as he thought it was.

Ironically, the disguised Kent, banished by Lear for defending the truth, is now pressed into service in the cause of justice. Kent appears as the loyal servant, deceiving his master so that he can protect the king from being destroyed by his own madness.

'And I'll go to bed at noon.'

After the trauma of the mock-trial, Lear begins to gain some insight into the world as it really is. Here he is exhausted and says he will take supper in the morning. The Fool replies that he will go to bed at noon. Some critics have interpreted these last words of the Fool as referring to a premonition of his coming death ('bed' meaning grave). Others see him to be commenting, in his typical way, upon Lear's crazy behaviour.

In this last scene in which the Fool participates his role steadily decreases, while that of Tom O'Bedlam grows. You might consider various reasons for this. Is it that the Fool's role is now inappropriate to Lear? He has warned him against folly, now Lear needs rest, not provocation to thought. It may have something to do with the growing importance of Tom O'Bedlam. Also, the Fool's disappearance from the play is deliberately shrouded in mystery: an ambiguous last line, an uncertain fate. Is the Fool here suffering from illness or terminal exhaustion? He manages a few quips and rhymes, but seems uninterested in the trial ('I took you for a joint-stool' shows his unwillingness to join in the fantasy) and eventually lapses into silence.

'When we our betters see bearing our woes, We scarcely think our miseries our foes.'

Edgar appears in his role as chorus here at the end of this scene. He comments on the action and draws the attention of the audience to the key points in what has happened. His function as chorus is reinforced by the use of soliloquy and rhyming couplets, which underlines the fact that he is not appearing as a part of the action, but as a commentator on it.

Edgar

Act 3 Scene 7

Gloucester is arrested and brought before Cornwall and Regan, where he is tied to a chair. Under questioning, Gloucester admits that he sent Lear away to Dover to be safe from Goneril and Regan and says he will see them punished for what they have done. A servant, outraged when Cornwall begins to put out Gloucester's eyes, fights with Cornwall in an attempt to stop him, but is killed by Regan. Gloucester is then blinded by Cornwall and thrown out of the castle, whilst Regan attends to a wound which Cornwall has received in the fight. Some servants take pity on Gloucester and bandage his bleeding face.

'Because I would not see
Thy cruel nails pluck out his poor old eyes'

Until now, Gloucester has been seen as a well-meaning but weak man. He protested at Kent being put in the stocks, but was intimidated by Cornwall into not doing very much about it. But he has now arranged for the care of Lear and in this scene he rounds on Regan and Cornwall. This is the start of Gloucester's rise in our estimation, which is further increased by his frightful blinding. He becomes a pitiful figure who represents the fate of all the weak but good-hearted people who seek to obstruct evil.

Gloucester's blinding is all the more vicious for being a part of the action

Blindness and sight

which is performed on stage, not reported, as is often the case in Shakespeare. Gloucester's references to eyes and seeing are both ironic and horrific, given what follows immediately after. Notice how the play's references to sight, seeing and eyes increase significantly in number as Gloucester's blinding approaches. In the same way, we find increasing references to divine justice and the gods after the blinding episode.

'Go thrust him out at gates, and let him smell
His way to Dover.'

Cordelia

Regan appears less openly aggressive than her sister, but is equally vicious. She pulls Kent's beard when he is tied up, then encourages Cornwall to further violence. She remains unmoved by the vicious blinding of Gloucester and urges Cornwall to put out his other eye: 'One side will mock another; th'other too', then has him thrown out to fend for himself. It is Regan who stabs the servant in the back as he fights with Cornwall to prevent further harm to Gloucester. Regan's jealousy of her sister's lustful relationship with Edmund mirrors the jealousy which both sisters feel towards Cordelia and grisly violence of this scene foreshadows the violence they later seek to wreak upon each other. The

42

wounding of Cornwall is a good example of an incident dealt with briefly and without emphasis that later assumes major importance.

Self-test questions Act 3

Uncover the plot
Delete two of the three alternatives given, to find the correct plot. Beware possible misconceptions and muddles.

Lear rages on the battlements/riverside/heath at the surrounding storm as Tom/Gloucester/the Fool tries to get him to shelter. Kent appears and persuades Lear to seek out a nearby hovel/inn/cave. Meanwhile Gloucester/France/Albany tells Edmund/Oswald/Curan that Burgundy/Cornwall/Lear has commandeered the castle. Edgar/Oswald/Gloucester says he has a letter which tells of a military power coming to revenge Lear. Edmund/Oswald/Curan decides to betray him.

In the storm Lear thinks about his past/the poor and homeless/killing himself. Kent/the Fool/Gloucester discovers Edmund/Edgar/Albany, disguised as Tom O' Bedlam, in a hovel. Tom says he is being punished for many sins/adultery/disobedience. Gloucester/Albany/France offers shelter; he says that Goneril and Regan now seek Lear's lands/imprisonment/death. Edmund/Edgar/Burgundy tells Cornwall about the parcel/locket/letter and is sent off to arrest his brother/uncle/father. Gloucester tells Edgar/Cornwall/Kent he sent Lear away to Dover to be safe from Goneril/Regan/Ophelia and Regan/Goneril/Cordelia. Gloucester is blinded by Cornwall/Edmund/Albany and thrown out of the castle, but not before a servant has wounded him. Servants get the Fool/Tom/Edgar to lead Gloucester.

Who? What? Why? When? Where? How?
1 Who first suggests to whom that Goneril and Regan want their father dead?
2 Where does Gloucester hide the letter?
3 Who tries to persuade Lear to come out of the storm?
4 How does Gloucester learn that Edmund has betrayed him?
5 Where does Kent advise the gentleman on the heath to go, and why?
6 How is Gloucester restrained during his meeting with Cornwall?
7 Which characters are involved in the mock-trial of Goneril and Regan?
8 Who suggests that Albany and Cornwall are no longer united, and to whom, and where?
9 Who interrupts the blinding of Gloucester and what happens to him?
10 Who goes into the hovel on the heath and what does this person do inside?

Who said that, and to whom?
1 '…things that love night/Love not such nights as these.'
2 'The younger rises when the old doth fall.'
3 'Pinion him like a thief, bring him before us.'
4 'We'll go to supper i'th'morning.'
5 'This cold night will turn us all to fools and madmen.'
6 '…from France there comes a power/Into this scatter'd kingdom.'
7 'I will have my revenge ere I depart his house.'
8 'He's mad that trusts in the tameness of a wolf, a horse's health, a boy's love, or a whore's oath.'
9 'I have lock'd the letter in my closet.'
10 'I have ta'en/Too little care of this.'

Open quotes
Identify the scene; complete the phrase; identify the speaker and the character being spoken to.
1   'First let me talk with this philosopher.'
2   'See't shalt thou never. Fellows, hold the chair.'
3   'Ha! Here's three on's are sophisticated; thou art the thing itself:...'
4   'Go thrust him out at gates, and let him smell...'
5   'Poor naked wretches, whereso'er you are,'
6   'Blow winds, and crack your cheeks! rage! blow!'
7   'Death, traitor! Nothing could have subdu'd nature/To such lowness...'
8   'Contending with the fretful elements: ...'
9   '... I would not see/Thy cruel nails pluck out his poor old eyes;'
10 'I am a man more sinn'd...'

Act 4 Scene 1

Edgar, still disguised as Tom O'Bedlam, meets Gloucester on the heath, being led by an old man. Gloucester says he will be guided by Tom and sends the old man away for clothes for him. Gloucester asks Tom to lead him to the edge of a high cliff at Dover.

'I have no way, and therefore want no eyes; I stumbled when I saw.'

Gloucester puts into words one of the play's central paradoxes but one which, like Lear, he recognises too late. His wanderings about the countryside, guided and cared for by what appears to be a rambling lunatic, are a powerful parallel for Lear's situation. For both men and for what they represent within the play, the paradox does not refer to actual vision but to self-knowledge, to understanding and to the acceptance of their part in the structures of order, reason and faith which guide the universe. Gloucester and Lear stand as lessons about humankind's proper place in the ordered society which flows from the figure of the divinely-appointed monarch.

Blindness and sight

'O gods! Who is't can say, "I am at the worst"? I am worse than e'er I was.'

Edgar is able to rejoice in his opening short soliloquy that he has reached the lowest point and that any change must be for the better. Immediately he sees his blind father, 'poorly led', regretting his offences to Edgar, and he realises that he has not even this consolation. So long as he is alive, able to say that 'this is the worst', then it is not the worst. Note the cruelty of the pagan gods. Edgar calls on them in his grief; more memorably,

Edgar

44

Gloucester sees them as killing us 'for their sport'. Edgar finds it increasingly hard to maintain the role of Poor Tom when confronted by his father's sufferings. Why do you think that there are so many asides (short comments to the audience) by him in this scene?

Fathers and children

Edgar's meeting with his blind father heralds a new stage in fathers/children relationships. Gloucester is helpless, as is Lear, and filial duty casts Edgar as his guide and preserver. His love for his father also brings agonies of grief, a contrast to previous reactions to paternal suffering.

Act 4 Scene 2

Goneril arrives at her husband's palace, where Oswald tells her that the Duke seems a changed man: he smiled on learning that Cordelia's army had landed, but was displeased to hear of Edmund's behaviour towards his father, Gloucester. Goneril tells Edmund to return to Cornwall and order him to prepare an army. She says that Oswald will take messages between them and they part in a way which suggests that they have deeper feelings for each other. After Edmund leaves, Albany arrives and condemns Goneril for what she has done to her father. She criticises him as cowardly and he replies that it is only because she is a woman that he does not physically attack her. A messenger brings a letter for Goneril from Regan, together with news of Gloucester's blinding and of Cornwall's subsequent death. In an aside, Goneril worries that Regan will try to steal Edmund from her, whilst her husband, the Duke of Albany, secretly declares that he will avenge the blinding of Gloucester.

'Oh! The difference of man and man.'

Goneril explicitly links the sexual attractiveness of Edmund with what she sees as his other manly qualities. For her, the greatest of these is the animal ruthlessness which she criticises her husband Albany for lacking. Lust and sexual desire are linked with the other forces of chaos. Edmund, as the product of lust, is associated with the forces of disorder, unrestrained passions, violence and adultery. Contrast this with the way the character of Cordelia is used in the play; unlike her sisters, she is not associated with sexual passions. Cordelia's love is filial; she honours her father even when he rejects her and she is associated with the political forces of order whilst her sisters are identified with baser feelings of all kinds.

'You are not worth the dust which the rude wind Blows in your face.'

After a long absence, Albany reappears as a man 'so chang'd' to denounce the wickedness of Goneril. He 'smil'd' at the thought of the French army landing to rescue Lear, to the puzzlement of Oswald and Goneril. Like many characters, he displays more wisdom as the play progresses.

'What have you done?
Tigers, not daughters, what have you perform'd?'

Blindness and sight

Goneril and Regan

The Duke of Albany criticises Goneril for her wickedness, calling her a devil and a fiend whom he should kill. Previously a moderate man, Albany is so moved by the evil of Goneril and Regan that he uses language full of violence and disgust. See how many words you can find in this speech that reflect the use of 'vile' in the first line. Goneril can see nothing but her own purposes and, fittingly in a play where references to insight and blindness abound, seems ignorant of how her own actions have turned her into a monster. Like her father, Goneril's lack of self-knowledge will ultimately be the cause of her own destruction and, also like her father, both she and Regan display their predominant character traits right from the start. Unlike Lear, however, neither of them shows any redeeming side to her nature.

'What news?'

This scene is full of information that transforms the plot from many different angles. Though the first three acts are full of action, the focus has been simply on the series of events that arise directly from the folly of Lear and Gloucester and the evil of some of their children. See how many surprises and messages for Albany or Goneril or both occur in this scene and assess their reactions.

Act 4 Scene 3

In the French camp, near Dover, we learn from Kent's questioning of a courtier that the King of France has had to return home urgently and that Cordelia has heard of Lear's treatment at the hands of her sisters. Kent reveals that Lear is in Dover, but will not see Cordelia because of the shame he feels at the way he treated her.

'Why the King of France is so suddenly gone back, know you no reason?'

Cordelia

In Act 1, scene 1, Cordelia declared that when she married she would give her husband half of all her love, not 'marry like my sisters,/To love my father all'. However, throughout the play we see her doing exactly that – loving her father unreservedly – and here Shakespeare removes the King of France from the climax of the action to emphasise this.

'Faith, once or twice she heav'd the name of "father" Pantingly forth, as if it press'd her heart'

The gentleman tells Kent of Cordelia's reaction to the letters she has received.

Love

This keeps Cordelia in the audience's mind, emphasises the kindness of her character and prepares the audience for her return to the action. Cordelia's almost holy qualities of innocent suffering and forgiveness are also emphasised by describing her tears as 'holy water' which fall from 'heavenly eyes'. Given that we see relatively little of Cordelia in the action, these references to her are telling, for they surround her otherwise vague character with an unworldly saintliness. This contrasts with the stubbornness we see in her in Act 1. On the other hand, some writers feel that Cordelia's change in perspective, like her father's, is brought about by suffering and pain and is not due to intrinsic character traits.

Act 4 Scene 4

Cordelia learns that her father has been seen wearing a crown of weeds and sends an officer to bring him to her. Her doctor says that rest and care will ease Lear's condition. A messenger brings news that the forces of Cornwall and Albany are marching towards them.

'Seek, seek for him, Lest his ungovern'd rage dissolve the life That wants the means to lead it.'

Order and reason

Cordelia correctly senses that Lear's life hangs by a thread, which his inner turmoil threatens to break. Without the means by which to conduct and guide ('lead') his own life – a sense of self-knowledge as well as his reason – he will die. Cordelia emphasises the importance of reason and order.

Act 4 Scene 5

In Gloucester's castle, Regan learns that Albany has been persuaded by Goneril to fight Cordelia's invading army. Regan tells Oswald that it was a mistake to let Gloucester live and tries to persuade him to let her read Goneril's letter to Edmund. She tells him that she knows that his mistress, Goneril, has designs on Edmund, but that she intends to have him for herself. She also tells Oswald that should he find Gloucester, he will be well rewarded if he kills him.

> 'It was great ignorance, Gloucester's eyes being out,
> To let him live; where he arrives he moves
> All hearts against us.'

Regan, as usual, accurately perceives the real situation and the real nature of other people. Note that, although Oswald is a trusted servant, he receives the official, politically correct version of Edmund's pursuit of his father: 'to dispatch/His nighted life.' Or does Regan expect Oswald, shrewdly political himself, to enjoy the irony of this interpretation of Edmund's bloody intentions? Edmund seems to be searching for Gloucester so that he may kill him to prevent him moving 'all hearts'.

> 'Why should she write to Edmund? Might not you
> Transport her purposes by word?'

The unpleasant imagery which surrounds the two daughters frequently emphasises their lack of tenderness and their treacherous ways. Here one of these 'unnatural hags', as Lear called them earlier, turns on the other in suspicion and tries to bribe Oswald. Regan then reveals to him her intentions – her 'darker purpose' – and it seems clear that the intrigue and treachery of the two women knows no bounds. They trust no-one, least of all each other.

Act 4 Scene 6

As they near Dover, Edgar tells the blind Gloucester that they have reached the coastal cliff he seeks. He pretends to leave him on the brink of the precipice. Gloucester says his farewells to the world and, thinking he will plummet to his death, throws himself forwards and falls. Pretending now to be a passer-by at the base of the cliff, Edgar helps Gloucester to his feet and congratulates him on a miraculous escape from death, saying that he saw him at the top of the cliff with a hideous demon. Gloucester says he will accept his blindness because the gods have saved him from death. Lear arrives, babbling madly, but Gloucester recognises his voice. As Lear raves about betrayal and hypocrisy, the search party arrives to take him to Cordelia. Lear runs off, and they follow him. Oswald arrives and, recognising Gloucester, declares that he will kill him, but Edgar interposes himself between them and kills Oswald when he attacks. Edgar reads the letters which Oswald was carrying and learns that Goneril wishes to marry Edmund and has asked him to kill her husband, Albany.

> 'How fearful
> And dizzy 'tis to cast one's eyes so low!'

This memorable description of Dover Cliff sees Edgar discarding the role and language of Poor Tom. 'Methinks you're better spoken', says Gloucester, but Edgar blames the old man's failing senses and takes charge of his interpretation of the world. The speech, full of telling images of reduced size, is directed at a blind man, of course, but is also part of a great Shakespearean tradition of compensating for the lack of scenic and lighting effects by evocative descriptions. The speech 'looking down' is paralleled by Edgar's terrifying descriptions after the fall of the height of the cliff and the devilish figure who (supposedly) parted from Gloucester at the cliff-top.

'O you mighty Gods! This world I do renounce'

Gloucester prepares to commit suicide, unable to bear the horrors of his life any longer. This episode emphasises the difference between the pathetic Gloucester and the tragic Lear. After his 'miraculous' escape from death, Gloucester learns stoicism and endurance, whilst Lear's tragic grandeur is beyond escape and calls forth more extreme reactions.

'Thy life's a miracle. Speak yet again.'

Edgar persuades Gloucester that he has fallen a great way down a huge cliff and that his escape from death is miraculous. This is another example of how Edgar, in various guises, influences the thinking of his father and of Lear and acts as a catalyst for developing and changing their perceptions.

Edgar

As a result of Edgar's deception, which he says he indulged in to cure his father of his despair at being blinded, Gloucester declares that he will bear his affliction from now on. By saving Gloucester from suicide, Edgar acts as an example of one of the play's great principles, that the will of God must be accepted and that humankind must accept its lot on earth.

Blindness and sight

'...they told me I was every thing; 'tis a lie, I am not ague-proof.'

Although Lear's speech is wild and raving, we can follow the sense of his bitterness at his fate and note that now the earlier arrogance of his character has passed. Although he is far from being a completely reformed character, we might wish to revise Regan's earlier observation in Act 1 that her father 'hath ever but slenderly known himself'. Or do we see within Lear's seeming ravings, as in the jibes of the Fool, the paradox that fools and madmen in the play often make more sense of the world than those who are deemed sane?

'Down from the waist they are centaurs, Though women all above'

Not for the first time, Lear connects his own misfortunes with the supposed promiscuity of women and the 'sulphurous pit' of hell. His attitude towards

King Lear

sexuality is evidence of the morally unhealthy state into which the world has fallen. Biblical echoes of the fall of humankind occur several times in the play. In this case, they appear as reminders of the base desires which tempt people into evil.

Gloucester: 'O! Let me kiss that hand.'
Lear: 'Let me wipe it first; it smells of mortality.'

The meeting between Gloucester and Lear on the beach at Dover is both dramatically important and moving. Although one is mad and the other blind, they recognise each other. They also recognise their situation as victims, but only partly understand the extent to which their torments have been brought upon them by their own actions. Nonetheless, the self-knowledge of both characters has improved since the play's beginning.

'Plate sin with gold,
And the strong lance of justice hurtless breaks'

With his new insight into the world, Lear recognises that the sins of the mighty

Order and reason

are more difficult to bring to justice than those of the weak and helpless. Edmund is the play's most striking example of sin plated with gold – one who conceals his treachery under the cloak of sincerity – others being Goneril and Regan. Lear himself, on his own journey of self-discovery, has come partly to appreciate how the trappings of power and majesty can conceal wrongdoing, disorder and injustice.

'When we are born, we cry that we are come
To this great stage of fools.'

Lear's sudden changes from sense to lunacy are well illustrated in his last

King Lear

speeches. His account of the need for patience is true and poetic. You might like to contrast his treatment here of Gloucester's sufferings with his earlier words to Gloucester: 'I remember thine eyes well enough', for example. He switches then to his 'delicate stratagem' and repeated commands to kill and soon departs in a crazy chase.

Madness

In this last scene before the restoration of Lear by Cordelia, the contrasts are brought out by many means. Note, for instance, the use of perfect blank verse for the sane and patient lines beginning 'If thou wilt weep my fortunes, take my eyes' in contrast to such manic lines as 'Then kill, kill, kill, kill, kill, kill!'

'Chill not let go, zur, without vurther 'casion'

Edgar now makes yet another change of role: into a peasant speaking what we may take to be broad Kentish. Why does he make this change? Is it to deceive Gloucester again or simply because he feels that Oswald deserves no better opponent? After the death of Oswald, he reverts to his own speech patterns. As later evidence shows, you would be mistaken to assume that the use of 'father' means that he has revealed his identity: clearly, it is just applied to an old man.

Act 4 Scene 7

Cordelia meets her father, who has just awoken. Lear at first thinks he has died and that she is just a spirit, but eventually realises he is alive and remembers something of his past. Lear leaves to rest further, leaving Kent and a gentleman to discuss the coming battle.

'I am bound
Upon a wheel of fire…'

Lear is reunited with Cordelia, having realised only slowly that he is not dead.

Order and reason

Lear has been redeemed through his suffering and repentance, echoing the Christian belief in forgiveness and in mercy in the afterlife. He knows himself to be a 'foolish fond old man' and asks Cordelia to 'forget and forgive' his behaviour. The importance of forgiveness and redemption is emphasised on several important occasions within the action.

The idea of Christian redemption through suffering is related to the play's theme of order and the importance of reason. Cordelia can be seen as representing that part of the natural order of the universe which strives for wholeness through love and forgiveness. The universal theme appears frequently throughout the play, as do references to divine intervention, the gods, stars and cruelty as the doing of devilish powers from the underworld.

'… to deal plainly,
I fear I am not in my perfect mind.'

King Lear

Ironically, it is Lear's increased self-knowledge here which marks the point at which he is recovering his sanity and the change from his earlier arrogant ignorance. Lear has come to see himself for what he is and as others see him. His character and role are – finally – the same.

Madness

Lear's confusion is inevitable. He understandably fears that he is 'not in his perfect mind', but once again the stage of madness is indicated clearly. 'The great rage', says the doctor, 'is kill'd in him.' His madness has always been based in anger and fury, and now it subsides.

Cordelia

Compare this with the way the character of Cordelia is handled. Her love for her father and her relatively few appearances combine to concentrate the audience's view of her. In view of the frequent references to pagan gods, Lear's belief that Cordelia is 'a soul in bliss' is significant.

'Be your tears wet? Yes, faith. I pray, weep not...'

Love

Cordelia's tears contrast with her father's refusal to come to terms with his own feelings. Lear still seems to feel that he is the one who has been the most wronged; his acceptance that Cordelia may have suffered at his hand is tempered, for she has only 'some' cause for complaint. Perhaps all that has changed in him is that his fury has abated – he now accepts his fate.

Blindness and sight

In spite of all the damage which Lear has brought upon himself and on others, he seems to inspire a quite unwarranted degree of loyalty and love from those around him. Cordelia, the Fool, Kent and Gloucester all recognise something good within him and risk their lives trying to help and serve him, even when he rejects them. In this respect the play affirms the Elizabethan perspective on Christian morality, both about the way humanity should respond to the suffering of others and about the importance of reason and order.

■ Self-test questions Act 4

Uncover the plot

Delete two of the three alternatives given, to find the correct plot. Beware possible misconceptions and muddles.

Gloucester asks the disguised Tom/Kent/Lear to lead him to a high cliff at Dover. Albany/Burgundy/Kent is displeased to hear of Edmund's behaviour towards his father and condemns Goneril/Ophelia/Desdemona for what she has done to Lear. She says he is weak/too indecisive/a coward. Goneril/Regan/Juliet worries that Juliet/Regan/Ophelia will try to steal Edgar/Oswald/Edmund from her. Albany/Kent/France decides he will avenge Gloucester's blinding. In Dover, Lear/Gloucester/Edgar will not see Cordelia because of shame. Cordelia/France/the doctor says that rest and care will ease Lear's condition. Goneril/Regan/Cordelia says the biggest mistake with Gloucester was to free him/let him live/keep him in England. Edgar/Edmund/Regan tells Gloucester he is at the cave/place/cliff he seeks. Gloucester throws himself forward and falls. Pretending to be a passer-by, Kent/Edgar/Edmund congratulates him on his escape from death. Lear meets Kent/Oswald/Gloucester. Oswald tries to kill Lear/Gloucester/Cordelia, but is himself killed by Edgar/Albany/Kent. The plot of Goneril/Regan/Cordelia to kill Albany/Lear/Regan is discovered by Edgar. Ophelia/Juliet/Cordelia meets Lear, who thinks he has died and that she is a spirit/demon/wandering soul.

Who? What? Why? When? Where? How?
1   What does the death of Cornwall demonstrate to Albany?
2   Who first speaks to Gloucester after his supposed fall down from the cliff?
3   Who meets Gloucester on the heath?
4   What favour does Gloucester ask of Tom O'Bedlam?
5   What reason is given for the King of France going home?
6   What prevents Albany from actually attacking Goneril?
7   What favour does Oswald refuse Regan?
8   According to Tom O'Bedlam, how many fiends have been in him at once?
9   What prevents Lear from coming to meet Cordelia when he is in Dover?
10   What mistake does Regan think was made about Gloucester?

Who said that, and to whom?
1   'You are not worth the dust which the rude wind/Blows in your face'
2   'Yours in the ranks of death.'
3   'A dog's obey'd in office.'
4   'It is the stars,/The stars above us, govern our conditions.'
5   'I live/To thank thee for the love thou show'dst the king.'
6   'I am bound/Upon a wheel of fire.'
7   'I'll love thee much …'
8   'Wisdom and goodness to the vile seem vile.'
9   '…the worst is not/So long as we can say "This is the worst".'
10   To thee a woman's services are due.'

Open quotes
Identify the scene; complete the phrase; identify the speaker and the character being spoken to.
1   'I have no way, and therefore want no eyes'
2   'Milk-liver'd man!'
3   'If you have poison for me, …'
4   'I am a very foolish fond old man,/Fourscore and upward, not an hour more or less;'
5   'Let copulation thrive; for Gloucester's bastard son…'
6   '…henceforth I'll bear/Affliction…'
7   'It will come,/Humanity must perforce prey on itself,'
8   'This world I do renounce…'
9   'Hadst thou been aught but gossamer, feathers, air,…'
10   'Thorough tatter'd clothes small vices…'

Act 5 Scene 1

Regan jealously asks Edmund if he has ever slept with her sister Goneril and he denies it. Goneril and Albany arrive and, in an aside, Goneril says she would rather lose the coming battle than see her sister win Edmund. Edgar enters, disguised, and talks privately with Albany. He gives Albany the letter he received from Oswald, tells him to read it in secret, then leaves. In a moment alone, Edmund confesses that he has sworn his love to both Goneril and Regan. He says that he needs Albany's leadership in the coming battle, but he hopes that Goneril will then kill him. After this, Edmund says he will see that Lear and Cordelia do not receive Albany's promised mercy.

**'But have you never found my brother's way
To the forfended place?'**

Regan seeks to know whether Edmund has slept with her sister. Throughout the play Edmund has displayed great panache as the opportunist villain and here, as elsewhere, he outwits the attempt to trap him by giving a typically deceiving answer. He plays off characters against each other and clearly feels that they are there simply to be used and discarded. In this, Edmund is as efficient as he is heartless: it is no surprise that he becomes the successful military leader of Cornwall's forces.

**'To both these sisters have I sworn my love;
Each jealous of the other'**

Edmund has no real feelings for Goneril, Regan or anyone else. He uses people purely for his own ends and will happily see them die as soon as they have ceased to be useful to him. He sees himself not so much above the law, as completely outside it. In his ambition – he is a brilliant opportunist – he behaves in a completely amoral way and appears to be blind to any concern about the right or wrong of what he is doing.

Act 5 Scene 2

Edgar leaves Gloucester under the shadow of a tree. As soldiers retreat around him, Gloucester is rejoined by Edgar with the news that they must flee because Lear and Cordelia have been captured.

**'What! In ill thoughts again? Men must endure
Their going hence, even as their coming hither:
Ripeness is all.'**

Edgar's reprimand to Gloucester expresses a central message of the play. When Gloucester could see the world he did not recognise the truth, but now that he is blind he is learning to understand. Now he must learn to accept the truth which has become clear to him.

Act 5 Scene 3

The captured Lear and Cordelia are content to go to prison, now that they are reunited. Edmund sends them away to prison, then sends a secret note after them with instructions that its contents are to be followed without mercy. Albany arrives with Goneril and Regan and demands the captives. Goneril and Regan argue about who will have Edmund, but Albany arrests him and Goneril for treason. As Edmund prepares to fight his challenger,

Regan is led away ill. Edgar appears, but cannot be recognised under his armour. He refuses to give his name, but Edmund says he will fight him anyway. Edmund is badly wounded and Albany reveals the letter to Goneril, who refuses to comment and leaves. Edmund confesses his crimes and Edgar reveals his identity and is welcomed by Albany. Edgar recounts what has happened to him and tells Albany that when he revealed his identity to Gloucester, the emotional shock was too much for the old man and he died.

A frantic messenger appears with a bloody knife, saying that Goneril has killed herself and confessed to killing Regan with poison. When the bodies are brought in, Edmund confesses that he has ordered the killing of Lear and the hanging of Cordelia. As Edmund is removed, Lear appears with the dead Cordelia in his arms, having killed the person who hung her. A messenger arrives with the news of Edmund's death and Albany restores Lear's kingdom to him but Lear suddenly says he thinks Cordelia is breathing, then faints and dies. Kent and Edgar agree to rule the kingdom together, although Kent says he does not expect to live much longer.

'No, no, no, no! Come, let's away to prison; We two alone will sing like birds i'th'cage.'

King Lear

Lear is so happy at being reunited with Cordelia that the idea of prison seems bearable. Notice how large a disaster it has taken to bring Lear to the point where at last he can begin to understand his own shortcomings, value others for what they truly are and recognise ingratitude. Even at the end of the play, Lear seems to feel no personal guilt over Cordelia's death. However, the idea of seeking blessings and forgiveness of each other both christianises the old pagan and affirms his belief in honesty, truth and love between father and daughter. His imagined life in prison removes him from political involvement: the old obsessions with power and revengeful gods are no more.

'Shut your mouth, dame, Or with this paper shall I stop it.'

Contrast Albany's reaction here towards his wife with the way she spoke to him in Act 4, where she accused him of being a 'milk-liver'd man'. There is an effective irony in Goneril's protestation that Edmund, the master of deception, was 'cozen'd' (cheated) by those honourable men, Albany and Edgar.

'In wisdom I should ask thy name;'

Edmund

Edmund has tried throughout the play to make events fit in with his version of reality. As truth and the emotions of others begin to unravel the situation his wiles have created, his conduct shows greater resignation and acceptance, even a hint of honour. He places himself at a disadvantage by not asking the name of his challenger, accepting him because of his war-like exterior. He faces his death, guilt, the identity of his opponent and the attempt to save Lear in the same spirit. Examine also how he speaks of the almost simultaneous deaths of himself and the two women he was 'contracted to'.

'Th'hast spoken right, 'tis true.
The wheel is come full circle; I am here.'

The image of a wheel occurs several times in the play. The Fool likens Lear's

Order and reason

decline to a great wheel running down a hill which others should avoid lest it drag them with it; Lear sees himself bound upon a wheel of fire as a device of perpetual torture. Here, Edmund uses the image that there is a structure and pattern to the events in the universe and that order will eventually re-impose itself on the forces of chaos. Edmund's comment here is therefore both an explanation for his downfall and a signal that his character is used to symbolise a particular position within the philosophical debate at the heart of the drama.

'… But his flaw'd heart,
Alack, too weak the conflict to support!'

Edgar here reports the death of his father. The death of Gloucester comes

The Earl of Gloucester

immediately before that of Lear and reinforces the link which has run throughout the play between these two men. Both of them have undergone similar degrees of suffering in their development, and both die because of extreme passion – the description of Gloucester's death could easily fit that of Lear. Both Gloucester and Lear reach greater self-knowledge through their torment and suffering.

Fathers and children

The culmination of the two fathers/children plots are remarkably similar. The evil children who wanted power bring about their own deaths in the pursuit of it. The old men are reconciled with their loving children and die in the knowledge or hope that they are still alive. Only Edgar (who 'disappeared' for so long) survives.

'Had I your tongues and eyes, I'd use them so
That heaven's vault should crack. She's gone for ever.'

Cordelia

Although the imagery surrounding Cordelia stresses her heavenly qualities, at the end she appears as pitifully mortal. The pain of her death is made more intense by its ambiguity, at least in the mind of Lear – he seems to know that she is dead but refuses to accept it. Lear dies still saying – or perhaps simply wishing – that she shows signs of life. Lear's final reference to Cordelia is both ironic and appropriate: 'Look on her, look, her lips,/Look there, look there!' Cordelia's silence echoes her refusal to speak at the start of the play – and her silence, once again, is more than Lear can bear.

King Lear

The image of Cordelia's corpse in the arms of the dead Lear also emphasises again the Christian perspective which runs through the play; only after suffering and forgiveness can death redeem the human spirit. Notice that it is Cordelia's inaction which has sparked events at the start of the play, to which Lear's fury and frustration is a reaction. Cordelia has been destroyed by the actions of the world, whilst Lear has destroyed himself.

While far from being completely transformed, Lear dies redeemed and forgiven, as befits references throughout the play. Shakespeare skilfully avoids a total change to Lear's character, perhaps in recognition of the frailty of humankind. Much debate has surrounded the issue of whether Lear dies thinking Cordelia is still alive. If she is, we may feel that his redemption affirms the power of her goodness; if not, we may sense an even stronger tragedy.

'And my poor fool is hang'd! No, no, no life!'

Love

Lear is grieving over Cordelia's body when he speaks this line. Given that 'fool' was a common term of affection in Shakespeare's day, it is unclear whether Lear is here referring to Cordelia, the Fool, or both. It is appropriate that these characters may be linked here, for the Fool is as loyal to Lear as his daughter, and has always been committed to telling the truth.

'Break, heart; I prithee, break!'

As Lear dies, it is appropriate that the noble Kent should be given these words.

The Earl of Kent

He has been a study in angry loyalty and has kept his allegiance to Lear from the beginning. Kent is unchanging; even his disguise only presented the world with another version of himself.

Whether Kent is speaking about Lear or himself is unclear; perhaps it is both. As the play moves to an end, his words draw attention to its message that suffering is an inescapable consequence of self-knowledge and spiritual enlightenment.

'I have a journey, sir, shortly to go;
My master calls me, I must not say no.'

Again, we are not sure whether Kent's reference to his 'master' refers to Lear or to God. Kent seems not to differentiate between the two, for his service to Lear has been absolute and unbending whether the world, or Lear himself, liked it or not. Kent's coming death marks another stage in the passing of the traditional order of the world which he and Albany have represented and reaffirms the play's message about the nobility of humankind when it endures suffering unquestioningly.

Order and reason

'The weight of this sad time we must obey; Speak what we feel, not what we ought to say.'

Fittingly, the last words of the play are spoken by Edgar, the character who

has done most to unmask evil and wrongdoing throughout the action. Edgar has had a key role in revealing truth of many kinds – he has exposed the rawer nature of humankind as Tom O'Bedlam and highlighted its chaos, suffering and degradation. He has punished Oswald and Edmund with death, and exposed evil to the light.

Edgar

■ Self-test questions Act 5

Uncover the plot

Delete two of the three alternatives given, to find the correct plot. Beware possible misconceptions and muddles.

Whilst alone, Albany/Edgar/Edmund confesses that he has sworn his love to both Goneril/Regan/Ophelia and Goneril/Regan/Cordelia. He says he hopes that Goneril/Regan/Desdemona will kill Albany/Cornwall/France and that he will have Kent/Lear/Gloucester and Goneril/Regan/Cordelia killed. The captured Lear is content to go to prison because he will be with Cordelia/the Fool/Tom. Edgar/Edmund/Cornwall sends a secret note that they are to be killed. Goneril and Regan argue about who will have Edgar/Albany/Edmund. Albany arrests Edmund/Edgar/Oswald and Goneril/Regan/Cordelia for treason. Edgar/Edmund/Cornwall is wounded by Edgar/Banquo/Cornwall in single combat and confesses his crimes. Tom/Edgar/Kent recounts what has happened to him and tells Lear/Cordelia/Albany that Gloucester has died. News arrives that Goneril/Juliet/Cordelia has killed herself and confessed to poisoning Ophelia/Regan/Cordelia. As Edmund is taken out, Banquo/Kent/Lear appears with the dead Cordelia in his arms. News arrives of Edmund's/Burgundy's/Oswald's death. Albany/Kent/Edgar restores Lear's kingdom to him. Kent/Lear/France says he sees Cordelia breathing, then dies. Kent/Albany/Macbeth and Edgar agree to rule the kingdom. Kent/Banquo/Lear says he does not expect to live much longer.

Who? What? Why? When? Where? How?

1 What is Regan afraid has occurred between Goneril and Edmund?
2 Who does Albany arrest?
3 Which characters are left to rule the kingdom at the end of the play?
4 Who seems indifferent to the news of Edmund's death?
5 What method does Lear use to try to tell whether Cordelia is really dead?

6　Who appears in disguise to give a letter to Albany?
7　How do Goneril and Regan die?
8　Why does Regan leave before the fight?
9　What reason does Edmund give Albany for his sending away of Cordelia and Lear after their capture?
10　Who comes to challenge Edmund and of what does he accuse him?

Who said that, and to whom?
1　'That's but a trifle here.'
2　'Before you fight the battle, open this letter.'
3　'The wheel is come full circle.'
4　'I arrest thee/On capital treason; and, in thy attaint,/This gilded serpent.'
5　'Know, my name is lost…'
6　'Shut your mouth, dame…'
7　'Jesters do oft prove prophets.'
8　'Ripeness is all.'
9　'Sick! O, sick!'
10　'I pant for life.'

Open quotes
Identify the scene; complete the phrase; identify the speaker and the character being spoken to.
1　'I have a journey, sir,…'
2　'O! you are men of stones…'
3　'By th'law of war thou wast not bound to answer…'
4　'O! Let him pass; he hates him…'
5　'The gods are just, and of our pleasant vices/Make instruments to plague us;'
6　'The weight of this sad time we must obey;…'
7　'But have you never found my brother's way…'
8　'Which of them shall I take?'
9　'Come, let's away to prison…'
10　'… but his flaw'd heart,/Alack too weak the conflict to support!'

■ How to write a coursework essay

Most of you will use your study of *King Lear* to write a coursework essay fulfilling the Shakespeare requirement for English and English Literature. In writing this essay, you must meet certain requirements. In particular, you must show awareness (though not necessarily at great length) of social and historical influences, cultural contexts and literary traditions. These can be covered in various ways. There are many comments in this guide on Renaissance views of order: this is part of the cultural and historical context. Though the play is far from being authentic historically, there are hints of pagan Britain which contrast with a historical background of castles and courts. The literary tradition of tragedy in the self-destruction of a great man is clearly relevant here.

It is also essential that you show considerable evidence of textual knowledge, even if the essay has a strong creative element. Types of response might include:

- scene analysis;
- character study;
- analysis of imagery and other linguistic features;
- dramatic effect of the play or one or more scenes;
- empathic response to character;
- reflections on a production.

If you are writing an analytical essay, the *most important* consideration is that you must develop an argument or explain a point of view throughout. There is little to be gained by saying what Lear says or does. What is important is that you relate his actions or words to your theme: the dramatic impact of the first scene, the theme of madness, his growing self-awareness or whatever you are writing about. Careful advance preparation will aid you in organising your theme or argument: making notes on the material, putting these notes in order, then working through two or three drafts of the essay. By doing this you can reach a decision on what each paragraph is to be about, as far as possible signalling this to the reader in the opening sentence, often called a *topic sentence* because it introduces the topic of the paragraph.

If you choose an imaginative/creative essay, the *first essential* is to reveal throughout your factual knowledge of the text and a soundly based interpretation of it. Mere imagination will not gain credit in textual study for GCSE English Literature.

The length of your essay will depend on the type of essay you write, your own wishes and your teacher's advice, but do bear in mind that it is only one of several pieces of coursework: there is no need for a 5000 word blockbuster.

Fathers and children

Analyse the presentation of the relationships between fathers and children in King Lear. *Discuss the ways in which this is related to the political developments of the play.*

- The first part of this question is straightforward, though requiring intelligent and knowledgeable development of opinion and evidence. It is probably a good idea to deal with this first, at some length, before tackling the more difficult second task.

- There are obviously two families to deal with: the royal family and the Gloucesters. Note the non-existence of mother figures: the only named female characters in the play are Lear's daughters. You can develop at length the overlapping themes of filial affection and barbarity. There is one loving and loyal daughter/son who is misunderstood and banished. In both families the others take advantage of paternal foolishness, though Edmund is active and Regan and Goneril reactive. The treacherous children are driven by material greed, have no regard for truth and are ready to cause the death of the father. Each father actually dies in the heartbreak of realising his errors and the love of one child.

- All of these points, and others, can be developed very successfully at length, with much use of reference and quotation. You should, however, make sure that the concept of 'loyalty' (and its opposite, of course) plays a large part in these explanations.

- When you turn to the political element of the question, there are two main areas for consideration. You should look at the political philosophy developed by Edmund, whether in his own voice or attributing it to Edgar. According to this philosophy, politics has become generational. We should set aside the follies and beliefs of the old and let the next generation produce a society without faith. Belief is to be succeeded by pragmatism.

- Especially, though, the play is about a patriarchal kingdom. Lear, in other words, is the father of his people, expecting obedience and loyalty, providing stability. He breaks his side of the bargain, destroying stability in a scene where political advantage and daughterly love are fatally confused. Goneril and Regan are simultaneously disloyal to king and father. In this sense characters like the Fool and Kent are the loyal children: parallels between both of them and Cordelia are frequent. Finally (and this could be the final stage of the essay, too) Edgar re-establishes filial loyalty and an orderly state. He, after all, has notably served both Lear and Gloucester as dutiful subject/son.

Madness

Discuss Shakespeare's presentation of madness in the play, considering such elements as:

- *how far Lear is advanced in madness at the start of the play;*
- *the varieties of madness in the play;*
- *the effects of madness on understanding the state of Mankind.*

- It is, of course, a perfectly sensible choice of essay to write on the character of Lear, with a consideration of his madness playing a major part, and that overlaps with this title, but they are distinctly different essays.

- A good way to start this essay would be to show how central madness is to the whole drama. In Act 3 the crazed Lear keeps company with the Fool and Edgar, in the disguise of Tom O'Bedlam. Madness becomes the norm. In such scenes as Act 3, Scenes 4 and 6, Kent and Gloucester desperately keep a hold on reality as characters strip off, accuse a joint-stool of treason, and discourse familiarly of spirits. Meanwhile the storm provides the sound effects for the destruction of the calm of civilisation. Madness is not uncommon in Shakespeare plays, but you should be able to show that in *King Lear* it is pivotal to the action and central to the effect.

- Having generalised about madness, you should consider the first explicit question: how mad is Lear in Act 1? This is interesting, with much material on both sides of the argument, and no 'right' answer. Folly and madness are often linked in the play and Lear is undoubtedly foolish, but you might well think that his authoritative behaviour at the outset does not fit with madness. Look for evidence of his power and control, over others, if not over himself. His first complaints against Goneril seem well enough reasoned, but you must also take note of the excess of fury that so quickly erupts at any dispute. He announces that his wits begin to turn early in Act 3, but the fear of going mad is there at the end of Act 1. Look at the language of human disgust he uses, the commentary of the Fool, etc.

- The second element is straightforward. Lear's madness is at its most spectacular in Act 3, but there is plenty of material elsewhere. Edgar's assumed madness is powerful and moving and can be charted without too much difficulty. The Fool is more difficult, but there is a definite feeling that, from controlled fooling, he increasingly inhabits an unhinged world of which he can make little sense, and by Act 3 there is little to separate fools and madmen. It is worth considering Gloucester, too, who, while not mad, spends Act 4 in an unreal world controlled by Edgar.

- In *King Lear* all inessentials are finally stripped away: riches, possessions, 'civilised' society. Understanding requires the awareness of Man, a 'poor, bare, forked animal'. So Lear, from his madness, comes to see how little he has understood both individuals (like Cordelia) and Mankind in general, with all its suffering and injustice. Madness helps to purge Lear of his selfish pride. Similarly, the assumed madness of Edgar helps to purge the state of the evil of Edmund, in particular.

- The play ends sadly, but calmly. Perhaps your essay could do so, too, pointing out the stillness and exhaustion that succeeds a time of evil and madness.

Key scenes

King Lear is particularly suited to an essay that deals specifically with one scene, there being so many memorable ones. Rather than concentrating on one scene, this section will give some general advice on approaching this question.

- **Choice of scene** Act 1, Scene 1, would be an excellent choice. Many of the key elements of the play and nearly all the key characters are present, it is a wonderfully dramatic scene and there is much to discuss on the state of Lear's mind. Act 2, Scene 4, is equally dramatic and crucial in plot terms, with Lear's flight to nowhere and the terror of imminent madness on him. From Kent in the stocks to the relentless arithmetic of Goneril and Regan, this is equally revealing about Lear's enemies. The storm scenes (Act 3, Scenes 2, 4 and 6) could be treated together for reasons given in the above section on **Madness**. There are many other possibilities (the blinding of Gloucester, the final scene, etc.); far too many to consider all of them.

- **Effect as drama** It is important to consider the effect of the scene on stage and having seen a production is an advantage. How should Lear appear on his first entrance? How do you make the storm outside reflect the storm inside men?

- **Importance of the scene itself** Examine key themes that are presented here: obviously madness in Act 3, for instance. Consider what is revealed about key characters: Act 2, Scene 4 is crucial in showing the strength of the Goneril/Regan alliance against Lear, despite differences of character and opinion. Study any features of particular interest: certainly all these scenes have any number of major speeches that are worth detailed analysis.

- **Relationship to the rest of the play** How does the scene mark an important stage in the action, prepare for future events or mark a stage in character development? For instance, Act 2, Scene 4, marks a crucial stage in character relationships. Things can never be the same again. Why not? Also, see what parallels and contrasts you can find to other scenes elsewhere.

- **Conclusion** Each of these sections, especially the second and third, is likely to be very long and the conclusion will depend upon the material covered. You should attempt, however, to make some sort of answer to the question: 'How does this scene help to make *King Lear* the sort of play it is?'

■ How to write an examination essay

Most of you will study *King Lear* as a coursework text, but it is useful to consider the approach to an examination essay on the play. The advice given below will be useful in helping you to approach any English Literature examination essays.

Before you start writing

- The first essential is thorough revision. It is important that you realise that even Open Book examinations require close textual knowledge. You will have time to look up quotations and references, *but only if you know where to look.*

- Read the questions very carefully, both to choose the best one and to take note of *exactly what you are asked to do.* Questions in an examination are likely to be on subjects similar to those considered in **How to write a coursework essay**, but you must make sure you know what is being asked: an astonishing number of candidates answer the question they *imagine or hope* has been asked. If you are asked to consider Shakespeare's presentation of the theme of parents and children, for instance, do not spend the whole time analysing Lear's relationships with his daughters and ignore the Gloucester sub-plot.

- Identify all the key words in the question that mention characters, events and themes, and instructions as to what to do, e.g. compare, contrast, comment, give an account, etc. Write a short list of the things you have to do.

- Look at each of the points you have identified and jot down what you are going to say about each.

- Decide in what order you are going to deal with the question's main points. Number them in sequence. Do not adopt a chronological approach unless you have a specific reason for doing so.

Writing the essay

- The first sentences are important. Try to summarise your approach to the question so the examiner has some idea of how you plan to approach it. Do not begin, 'Lear finally goes mad when he is refused his train of knights by both Regan and Goneril and so rushes from Gloucester's castle to face the storm on the heath.' A suitable opening for an essay on madness might be, 'Shakespeare examines the theme of madness in many different forms in *King Lear*: assumed madness, professional nonsense and true insanity. Some characters are driven to the brink of madness and others are led to greater understanding by the loosening of the controls of conventional reason.' Jump straight into the essay, do not waste time at the start. A personal response will be rewarded, but you must always answer the question: as you write the essay *refer back to your list of points.*

- Answer *all the question.* Many students spend all their time answering just one part of a question and ignoring the rest. This prevents you gaining marks for the parts left out. In the same way, failing to answer enough questions on the examination is a waste of marks which can always be gained most easily at the start of an answer.

- There is no 'correct' length for an essay. What you must do is spend the full time usefully in answering all parts of the question (spending longer than the allocated time by more than a few minutes is dangerous). Some people write faster than others: they don't always get the best marks!

- Take care with presentation, spelling and punctuation. It is generally unwise to use slang or contractions (e.g. 'they've' for 'they have').

- Use quotation or paraphrase when it is relevant and contributes to the quality and clarity of your answer. References to events often do not need quotation, but it is impossible to convey, for instance, the violence of Lear's fury or the shameless evil of Edmund without some evidence of their own words. In any case, *extended* quotations are usually unhelpful, and padding is a waste of time.

Self-test answers Act 1

Uncover the plot

Two of King Lear's daughters are married: Goneril to the Duke of Albany; Regan to the Duke of Cornwall. The King of France and the Duke of Burgundy both seek to marry Cordelia. Goneril and Regan tell Lear they love him more than anything else but Cordelia refuses. Lear becomes furious and disowns Cordelia. Kent, who argues against this, is banished. Burgundy refuses to accept Cordelia, but France does and they go off to France together. Goneril and Regan say they will deal with Lear because he has become infirm and troublesome. The Earl of Gloucester's illegitimate son Edmund has a forged letter. He says he will use this to steal his brother's lands. It contains plans about murdering Gloucester. Edmund tells Edgar to hide. Goneril ensures that her servants are rude to Lear and his knights. Kent successfully gets back into Lear's court because he is disguised. Goneril becomes angry at the behaviour of Lear's knights. Lear says he will leave. Albany is unhappy about this. Meanwhile, the Fool ridicules Lear for his lack of wisdom.

Who? What? Why? When? Where? How?

1   Kent, whilst in disguise, tells Lear he is 48 years old
2   She says she fears that with their strength Lear will enforce his every whim and complaint, and that in his present dotage this will threaten all their lives
3   Gloucester
4   The Fool tells him the answer - he is Lear's shadow
5   Oswald is told to behave this way towards Lear, by Goneril
6   Fifty
7   He trips him up and verbally abuses him for being disrespectful to Lear
8   The Fool, who complains that he is whipped by Lear's daughters for speaking the truth, whilst Lear has him whipped for lying
9   The two halves of an egg
10 He hopes still to serve Lear

Who said that, and to whom?

1   Goneril, talking to Lear
2   France, when accepting Cordelia's hand in marriage
3   Gloucester, asking to read the letter which Edmund says he has from Edgar
4   Lear, talking to nobody in particular, but answered by the Fool
5   Kent, advising Lear not to divide his kingdom
6   Edgar, having heard that his father Gloucester is angry with him from Edmund
7   Lear, talking to Cordelia when she will not make a speech about how much she loves him
8   Kent, returning in disguise to the court of Lear, intending to serve him again
9   Edmund, in a soliloquy about his defiance of the laws of man
10 Lear, talking to Kent, Cornwall, Albany, Goneril, Regan and Cordelia

Open quotes

1   'if it be nothing, I shall not need spectacles.' Gloucester, asking Edmund about the letter he is pretending to conceal, in Act 1, scene 2
2   'that thou wast born with.' The Fool, talking to Lear in Act 1, scene 4 about why the king is a fool
3   'yet he hath ever but slenderly known himself.' Regan, discussing Lear with Goneril in Act 1, scene 1
4   'That it had it head bit off by it young.' The Fool, talking to Lear in Act 1, scene 4

5   'To have a thankless child!' Lear, talking to Albany and Goneril in Act 1, scene 4
6   'thou show'st thee in a child,/Than the sea-monster.' Lear, speaking to Albany about Goneril (in her presence) in Act 1, scene 4
7   '... as my sister,/And prize me at her worth.' Regan, talking to Lear in Act 1, scene 1
8   'often the surfeits of our own behaviour, we make guilty of our disasters the sun, the moon, and stars.' Edmund, talking to Gloucester in Act 1, scene 2
9   'speaking true, thou'lt have me whipp'd for lying; and sometimes I am whipp'd for holding my peace.' The Fool, complaining to Lear in Act 1, scene 4
10 'Freedom lives hence, and banishment is here.' Kent, talking to Lear after he has been banished in Act 1, scene 1

▓ Self-test answers Act 2

Uncover the plot

Edmund tells Edgar that he must run away, and fakes a sword fight to help him escape. After wounding himself, Edmund tells Gloucester that Edgar attacked him because he would not agree to join a murder plot. Gloucester says Edgar is to be killed and Edmund will be his legitimate heir. Cornwall takes Edmund into his service. Kent beats Oswald for being a rogue and a scoundrel and Cornwall has him put in the stocks for this. Edgar decides to disguise himself. He will be Tom, a wandering madman. Lear is angry to see Kent in the stocks, and when Regan and Cornwall at first say they will not see him. They say they are too tired and ill. Regan says Lear should return to Goneril. Goneril says, with Regan, that Lear should dismiss his men. Lear is furious and leaves even though a storm is developing. Gloucester pleads with Goneril and Regan to house Lear and his men but they and Cornwall say that Lear must suffer for his own foolishness.

Who? What? Why? When? Where? How?

1   The Duke of Cornwall is Gloucester's 'worthy arch and patron'
2   In the hollow of a tree
3   One hundred
4   He goes to sleep
5   Gloucester, who says that Lear will punish Kent if he has given any offence, but will be insulted if his official messenger is punished like a common thief
6   Edmund
7   She says she has had letters from both Lear and Goneril which show that there are 'differences' between them, about which they need Gloucester's advice
8   Two days
9   He kneels and asks her whether she thinks it becomes him to beg forgiveness, food, bed and clothing
10 He gives himself a wound on the arm and uses this as evidence

Who said that, and to whom?

1   Cornwall, praising Edmund for defending Gloucester against Edgar and taking him into his service. Act 2, scene 1
2   Kent, talking to Cornwall in Act 2, scene 2 about Oswald
3   Lear, to Regan just before she sides against him with Goneril in Act 2, scene 4

4   Cornwall to Gloucester, after Lear has raged out into the storm at the end of Act 2, scene 4
5   Lear, to Cornwall, Goneril and Regan in Act 2, scene 4
6   Lear, beginning to answer Regan's question about why he needs his knights. Act 2, scene 4
7   Edmund, talking to Edgar and betraying him in Act 2, scene 1
8   Kent, in reply to Cornwall who has just called for the stocks in Act 2, scene 2
9   Lear, in reply to the news that Cornwall and Regan are too tired and sick to see him. Act 2, scene 4
10 Oswald, to Kent, after Kent has insulted him. The start of Act 1, scene 2

Open quotes
1   'Will not be rubb'd nor stopp'd.' Gloucester, sympathising with Kent about his imprisonment in the stocks in Act 2, scene 2
2   'Must be their schoolmasters.' Regan, talking to Gloucester at the end of Act 2, scene 4
3   'Age is unnecessary: on my knees I beg/That you'll vouchsafe me raiment, bed, and food.' Lear, mockingly to Regan when she suggests to him in Act 2, scene 4 that he make up his quarrel with Goneril
4   'doth affect/A saucy roughness.' Cornwall, in reply to Kent's plain speaking in Act 2, scene 2
5   'stands on the very verge/Of her confine.' Regan, explaining to Lear why he should be kinder to Goneril. Act 2, scene 4
6   'something yet: Edgar I nothing am.' Edgar, in the soliloquy which forms all of Act 2, scene 3
7   'and daub the wall of a jakes with him.' Kent, talking to Cornwall about Oswald in Act 2, scene 2
8   'I'th'mire.' Kent's insulting reply to Oswald, at the start of scene 2 in Act 2
9   'Than stands on any shoulder that I see/Before me at this instant.' Kent, talking to Cornwall and his followers in Act 2, scene 2
10 'lest it break thy neck with following.' The Fool, advising Kent who is in the stocks in Act 2, scene 4

Self-test answers Act 3

Uncover the plot

Lear rages on the heath at the surrounding storm as the Fool tries to get him to shelter. Kent appears and persuades Lear to seek out a nearby hovel. Meanwhile Gloucester tells Edmund that Cornwall has commandeered the castle. Gloucester says he has a letter which tells of a military power coming to revenge Lear. Edmund decides to betray him.

In the storm Lear thinks about the poor and homeless. The Fool discovers Edgar, disguised as Tom O' Bedlam, in a hovel. Tom says he is being punished for many sins. Gloucester offers shelter; he says that Goneril and Regan now seek Lear's death. Edmund tells Cornwall about the letter and is sent off to arrest his father. Gloucester tells Cornwall he sent Lear away to Dover to be safe from Goneril and Regan. Gloucester is blinded by Cornwall and thrown out of the castle, but not before a servant has wounded him. Servants get Tom to lead Gloucester.

Who? What? Why? When? Where? How?

1 Gloucester, talking to Kent
2 He keeps it locked in his closet
3 Kent, then Gloucester
4 From Regan, who taunts Gloucester with this information when he calls out for Edmund after his blinding
5 He tells him to go to Dover and take news of events to Cordelia, who is there
6 His arms are tied, then he is also bound to a chair
7 Lear, Edgar, the Fool, Kent
8 Kent, when talking to a gentleman on the heath
9 A servant, who fights with Cornwall but is killed with a sword by Regan
10 Only the Fool, who runs out on discovering Tom O'Bedlam inside

Who said that, and to whom?

1 Kent, speaking to the Fool and Lear in Act 3, scene 2
2 Edmund, in a soliloquy at the end of Act 3, scene 3
3 Cornwall, talking about Gloucester to his servants in Act 3, scene 7
4 Lear says this to the Fool and Kent in Act 3, scene 6
5 The Fool, talking to Edgar and Lear during the storm in Act 3, scene 4
6 Kent tells this news to the Gentleman he meets on the heath in Act 3, scene 1
7 Cornwall, talking to Edmund about Gloucester at the start of scene 5 in Act 3
8 The Fool, speaking to Lear and Edgar before the mock-trial in Act 3, scene 6
9 Gloucester, tragically confiding in Edmund in Act 3, scene 3
10 Lear, in a soliloquy during the storm in Act 3, scene 4

Open quotes

1 'What is the cause of thunder?' Lear, talking to Tom O'Bedlam in Act 3, scene 4
2 'Upon these eyes of thine I'll set my foot.' Cornwall, talking to Gloucester before he blinds him in Act 3, scene 7
3 'unaccommodated man is no more but such a poor, bare, forked animal as thou art.' Lear, talking to Edgar in Act 3, scene 4
4 'His way to Dover.' Regan, talking to servants after the blinding of Gloucester at the end of Act 3
5 'That bide the pelting of this pitiless storm,/How shall your houseless heads and unfed sides,/Your loop'd and window'd raggedness, defend you/From seasons such as these?' Lear, in a soliloquy in Act 3, scene 4
6 'You cataracts and hurricanoes, spout/Till you have drench'd our steeples, drown'd the cocks!' Lear calls down the forces of heaven against those he thinks have wronged him. Act 3, scene 2
7 'but his unkind daughters.' Lear, talking to Kent about Tom O'Bedlam in Act 3, scene 4
8 'Bids the wind blow the earth into the sea ...' The Gentleman tells Kent of the whereabouts of the king at the start of Act 3, scene 1
9 'Nor thy fierce sister in his anointed flesh/Rash boarish fangs.' Gloucester, telling Regan why he helped Lear escape to Dover in Act 3, scene 7
10 'against than sinning.' Lear, speaking more to himself than those around him in Act 3, scene 2

■ Self-test answers Act 4

Uncover the plot

Gloucester asks the disguised Tom to lead him to a high cliff at Dover. Albany is displeased to hear of Edmund's behaviour towards his father and condemns Goneril for what she has done to Lear. She says he is a coward. Goneril worries that Regan will try to steal Edmund from her. Albany decides he will avenge Gloucester's blinding. In Dover, Lear will not see Cordelia because of shame. The doctor says that rest and care will ease Lear's condition. Regan says the biggest mistake with Gloucester was to let him live. Edgar tells Gloucester he is at the cliff he seeks. Gloucester throws himself forward and falls. Pretending to be a passer-by, Edgar congratulates him on his escape from death. Lear meets Gloucester. Oswald tries to kill Gloucester, but is himself killed by Edgar. The plot of Goneril to kill Albany is discovered by Edgar. Cordelia meets Lear, who thinks he has died and that she is a spirit.

Who? What? Why? When? Where? How?

1 That heaven continues to judge the affairs of human kind on earth below
2 Edgar
3 Edgar
4 That he lead him to a high cliff at Dover
5 Important unfinished state business called him back to France
6 Only the fact that she wears the shape of a woman
7 She asks him to allow her to unseal and read a letter belonging to Goneril which he carries
8 Five
9 Kent says it is because Lear feels ashamed at the way he has treated her
10 She thinks that it was a mistake to let him live after blinding him, for now wherever he goes he 'moves all hearts' against her and her allies

Who said that, and to whom?

1 Albany, speaking to Goneril in Act 4, scene 2
2 Edmund, talking to Goneril in Act 4, scene 2
3 Lear, talking to Gloucester in Act 4, scene 6
4 Kent, talking to a Gentleman in Act 4, scene 3
5 Albany, on hearing from the messenger, in Act 4, scene 2, that Gloucester's blinding was as a result of Edgar informing on him
6 Lear, talking to Cordelia in Act 4, scene 7
7 Regan, trying to persuade Oswald to let her read Goneril's letter in Act 4, scene 5
8 Albany, talking to Goneril in Act 4, scene 2
9 Edgar, speaking in an aside at the sight of the blinded Gloucester in Act 4, scene 1
10 Goneril, talking to herself about Edmund in Act 4, scene 2

Open quotes

1 'I stumbled when I saw.' Gloucester, talking to an old man in Act 4, scene 1
2 'That bear'st a cheek for blows, a head for wrongs.' Goneril, criticising Albany in Act 4, scene 2 for cowardice
3 'I will drink it./I know you do not love me.' Lear, talking to Cordelia in Act 4, scene 7
4 'And, to deal plainly,/I fear I am not in my perfect mind.' Lear, talking to Cordelia in Act 4, scene 7

5 'Was kinder to his father than my daughters/Got 'tween the lawful sheets.' Lear, talking to Gloucester in Act 4, scene 6

6 ''till it do cry out itself/"Enough, enough," and die.' Gloucester, telling Edgar in Act 4, scene 6 that he will bear his fate

7 'Like monsters of the deep.' Albany, whilst condemning Goneril for her behaviour in Act 4, scene 2

8 'and in your sights/Shake patiently my great affliction off.' Gloucester, talking to himself (as he thinks) in Act 4, scene 6

9 'So many fathom down precipitating,/Thou'dst shiver'd like an egg.' Edgar, talking to Gloucester in Act 4, scene 6

10 'do appear;/Robes and furr'd gowns hide all.' Lear, talking to Gloucester in Act 4, scene 6

■ Self-test answers Act 5

Uncover the plot

Whilst alone, Edmund confesses that he has sworn his love to both Goneril and Regan. He says he hopes that Goneril will kill Albany and that he will have Lear and Cordelia killed. The captured Lear is content to go to prison because he will be with Cordelia. Edmund sends a secret note that they are to be killed. Goneril and Regan argue about who will have Edmund. Albany arrests Edmund and Goneril for treason. Edmund is wounded by Edgar in single combat and confesses his crimes. Edgar recounts what has happened to him and tells Albany that Gloucester has died. News arrives that Goneril has killed herself and confessed to poisoning Regan. As Edmund is taken out, Lear appears with the dead Cordelia in his arms. News arrives of Edmund's death. Albany restores Lear's kingdom to him. Lear says he sees Cordelia breathing, then dies. Kent and Edgar agree to rule the kingdom. Kent says he does not expect to live much longer.

Who? What? Why? When? Where? How?

1 That they have committed adultery together
2 Edmund and Goneril
3 Kent and Edgar, supported by Albany
4 Albany
5 He asks for a mirror to see if it will mist up because she is breathing
6 Edgar
7 Regan is poisoned by Goneril, who then takes her own life with a knife
8 Because she is feeling unwell
9 He says he has sent them somewhere safe under guard, so that Albany can see them at his leisure the day after, or later
10 Edgar, who accuses Edmund of being a traitor

Who said that, and to whom?

1 Albany, speaking to an officer who has brought news of Edmund's death in Act 5, scene 3
2 Edgar, talking to Albany in Act 5, scene 1
3 Edmund, talking to Edgar in Act 5, scene 3
4 Albany, talking to Edmund and Goneril in Act 5, scene 3
5 Edgar, answering the herald's query in Act 5, scene 3
6 Albany, talking to Goneril in Act 5, scene 3
7 Regan, talking to Goneril and Albany in Act 5, scene 3

8   Edgar, talking to Gloucester in Act 5, scene 2
9   Regan, dying from the poison Goneril has given her in Act 5, scene 3
10   Edmund, to Albany in Act 5, scene 3

Open quotes

1   'shortly to go;/My master calls me, I must not say no.' Kent, speaking at the
     end of the play about his coming death. Act 5, scene 3
2   'Had I your tongues and eyes, I'd use them so/That heaven's vault should
     crack.' Lear, entering with the dead Cordelia in his arms in Act 5, scene 3
3   'An unknown opposite; thou art not vanquish'd,/But cozen'd and beguil'd.'
     Goneril, talking to Edmund after he is defeated in single combat in Act 5,
     scene 3
4   'That would upon the rack of this tough world/Stretch him out longer.' Kent,
     in Act 5, scene 3, speaking to Edgar about the death of Lear
5   'The dark and vicious place where thee he got/Cost him his eyes.' Edgar,
     talking to Edmund after mortally wounding him in single combat in Act 5,
     scene 3
6   'Speak what we feel, not what we ought to say.' Edgar, speaking the final
     lines of the play. Act 5, scene 3
7   'To the forfended place?' Regan, asking Edmund in Act 5, scene 1 if he has
     ever committed adultery with Goneril
8   'Both? One? Or neither? Neither can be enjoy'd/If both remain alive.' Edmund,
     in a soliloquy in Act 5, scene 1
9   'We two alone will sing like birds i'th'cage.' Lear, talking to Cordelia after their
     capture in Act 5, scene 3
10   ''Twixt two extremes of passion, joy and grief,/Burst smilingly.' Edgar, talking
     to Edmund about Gloucester in Act 5, scene 3